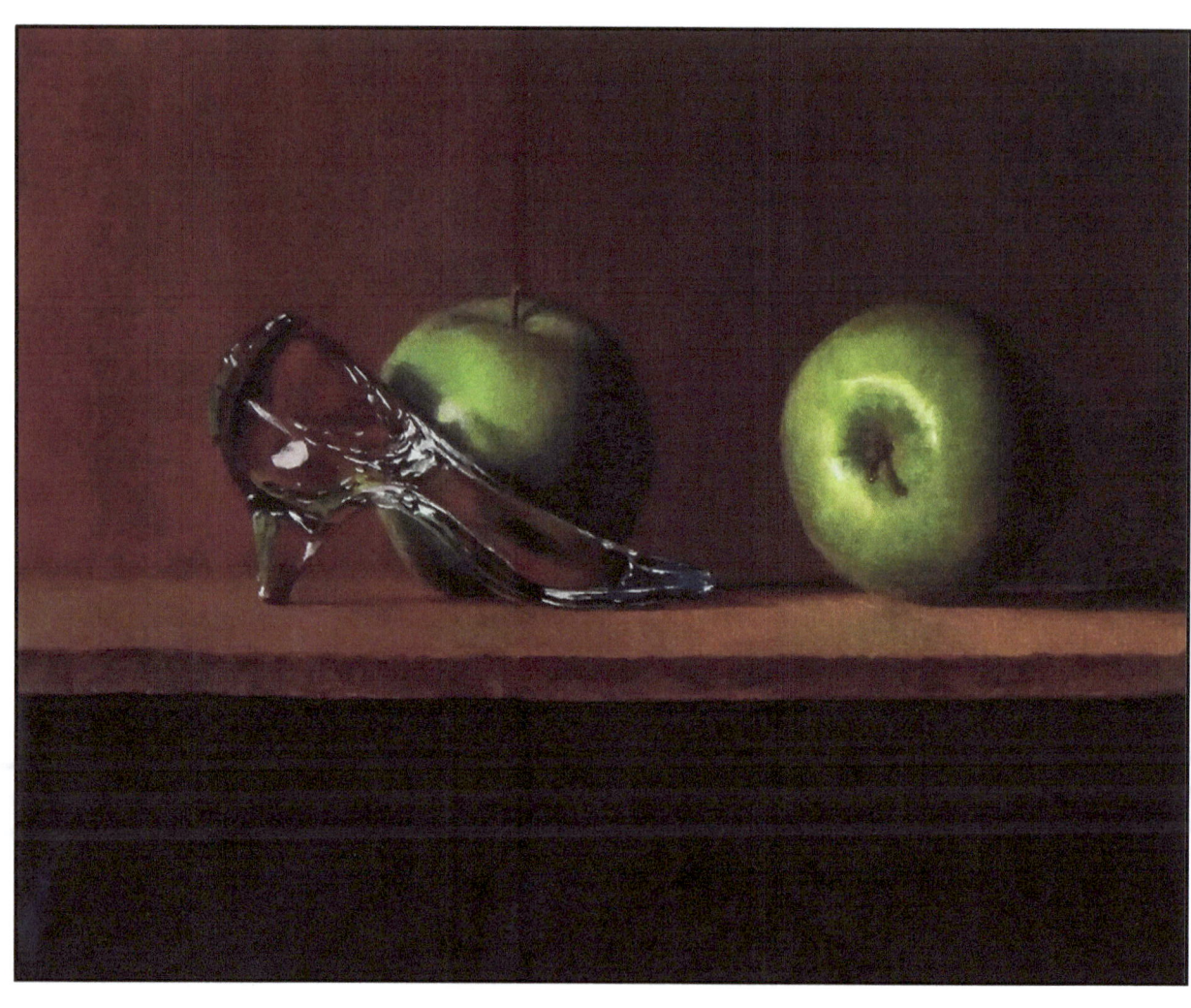

MIKE RIDER
Paintings and Drawings

Published by Mike Rider.

- ISBN-13: 978-1517681807
- ISBN-10: 1517681804

Page 2 image:
Tempted by Eileen
oil on board
11" x 14"
2010

Page 5 image:
Ephemeral Tranquility
oil on board
18" x 24"
2013

A special thank you to my wife Sharon,
for her invaluable love and support.

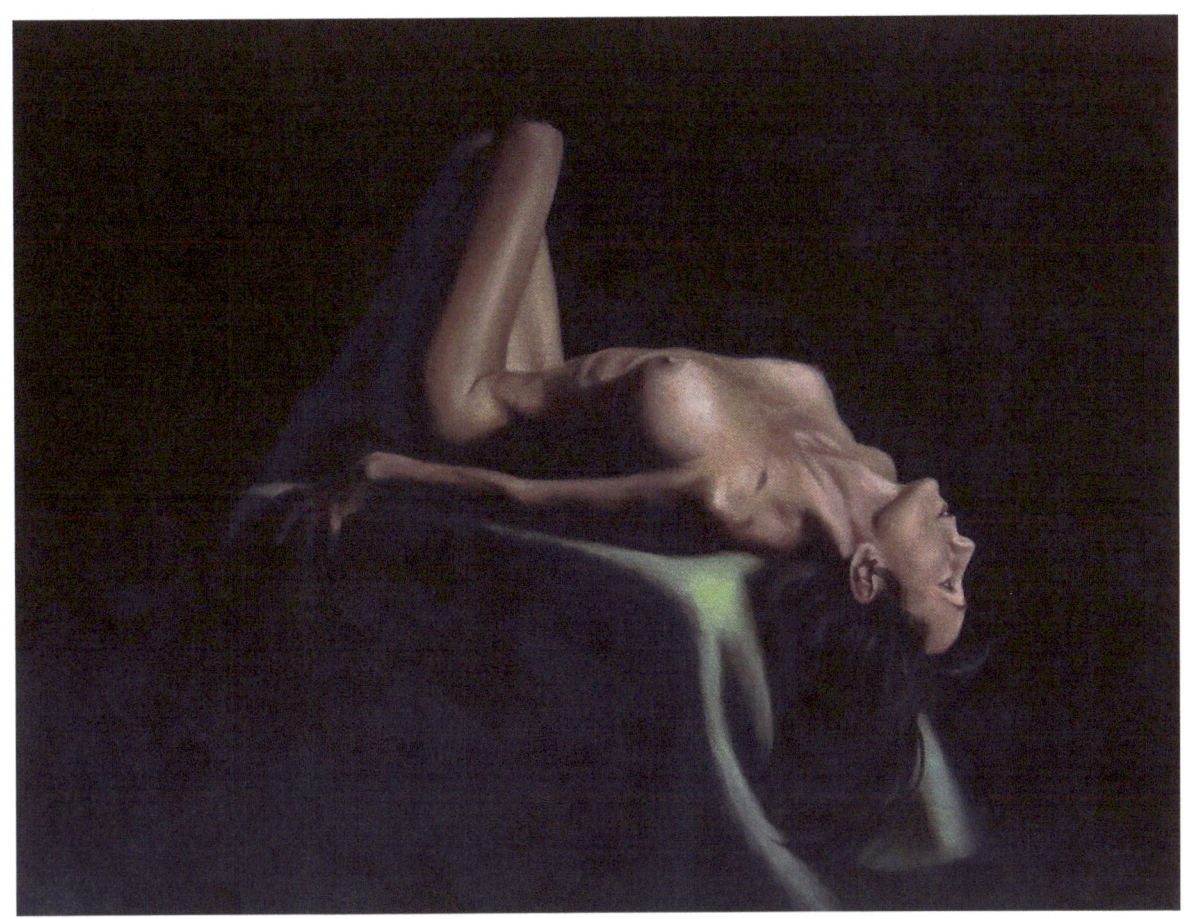

CONTENTS

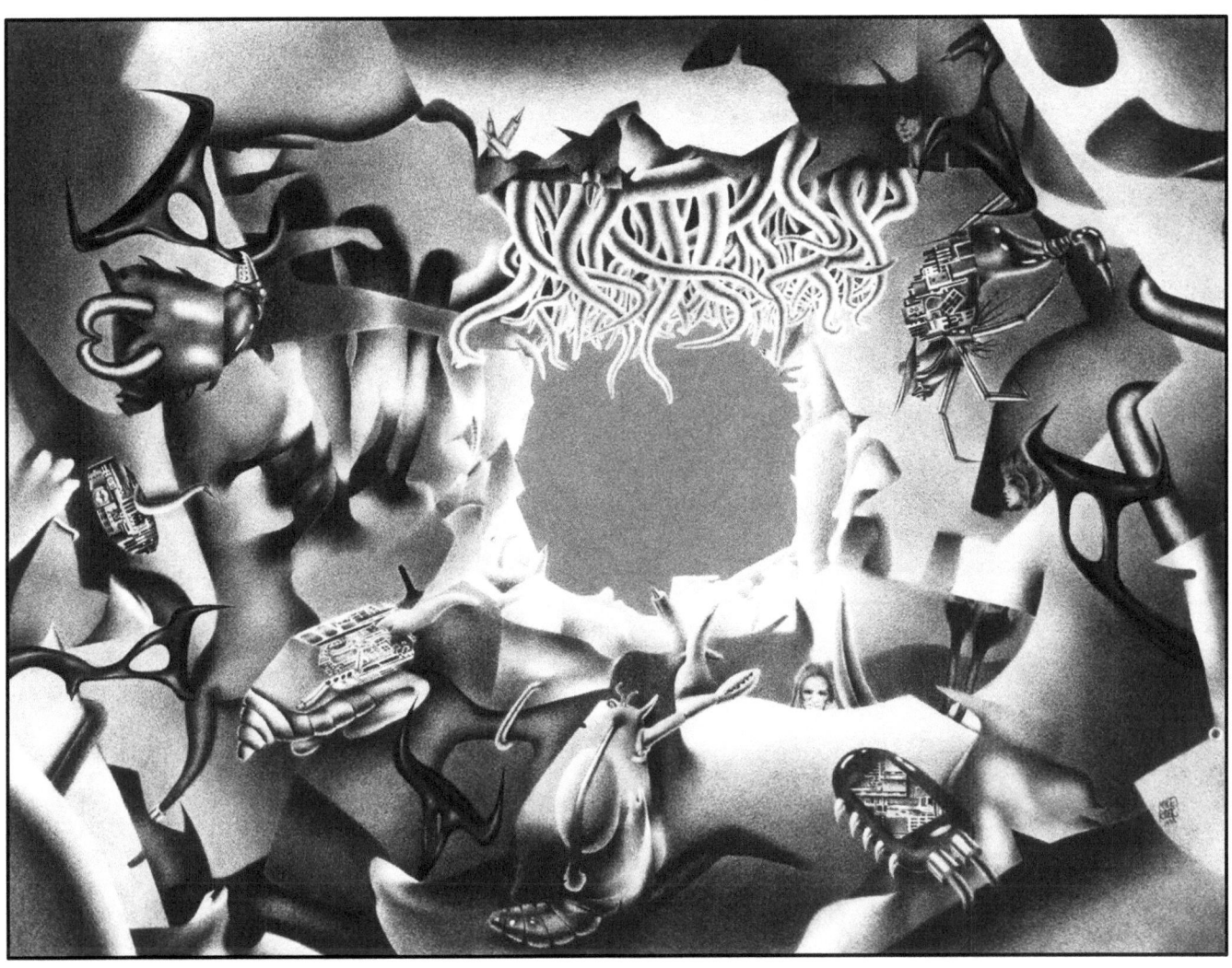

Accession
graphite and color pencil
15" x 22"
1989

Introduction by *Mike Rider*

Why publish this book now? A good question to ask.

Before 2000 I had been largely working in a surrealistic style. For me, it was a purely visual reality with it's own independent existence. My art was a gaze into this alternate world, more or less. The drawing shown above, *Accession*, is probably the best representative of that period.

For specific exhibition venues, I still occasionally work in a less abstract form of surrealism as exemplified by "Until…" (p. 22).

As time went on, I started to question my art as to what I was communicating and whether viewers were "getting it". As my own interest in the subject waned I knew it was time for a change.

I started looking at my life experience for subject matter. What I have most in common with the rest of humanity is the world in which we all exist. Every one of us has a unique take on how we experience our reality. These are the images I chose to paint and draw. Technique aside, art is simply a matter of an artist's perspective, imagination, and composition.

The work shown here started around 2000, the turn of the century. If asked, I would say that I work in a representational style. I do not consider it to be realism. With the exception of portrait commissions, I never felt obligated to simply duplicate my subject. For instance, if a reference photo for a commission was overexposed, I might reconstruct the missing values to make the image more real and less like a photograph. While visiting some of the landscape locations, one might see a dead tree or two that I chose not to include.

The paintings and drawings in this book were produced between 2000 and 2015. Of all the drawings and paintings produced during this period, I have selected only what I consider to be my very best work.

Many of these paintings and drawings have stories.

I've pitched our tent around 25 feet from *Workman Creek* more times than I can remember. It was my favorite creek-side camping spot for over thirty years. There's nothing like falling asleep to the sound of a trickling stream. One night we arrived to find thousands of daddy long-legs bobbing up and down as far as our flashlight could shine. The rain was drizzling. They were everywhere. We fell asleep looking at their moonlit bouncing spider shadows crawling up the outside of our tent. It was eerie. In the morning they were gone.

My dear friends Conan and Cricket who are portrayed in *Break Time* both passed away last year. They were family. If there is a cat and dog Valhalla they are up there now, fighting over the best nap spots. It was hard to keep Conan out of my paintings since he was usually in and out the water. He was often the source of the most beautiful ripples and reflections.

The Sonoran Desert mysticism described by *Carlos Castaneda* can be felt deep in the canyons of *Tortilla Creek*. It flows out of the border of the legendary Superstition Mountains. The gateway is the boulder-filled cathedral of Peters Canyon. Not a leisurely hike. If you venture further, best to stay on the Creek and ignore the siren-like lure of the hypnotic stone landscape that surrounds you. Or join the ranks of those who wandered into the Superstitions and never found their way out.

Mike Rider
October 2015

Drawings

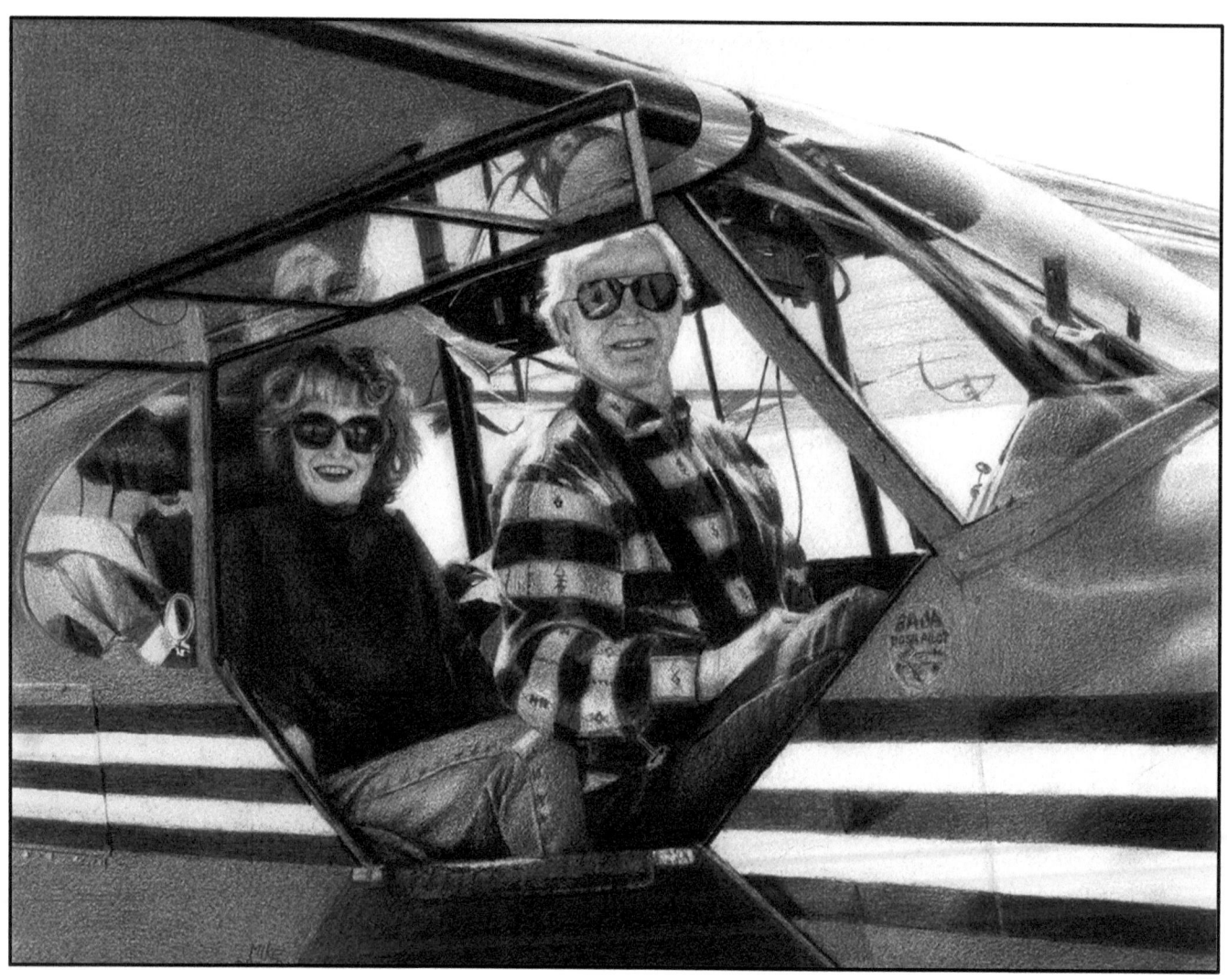

Joan and Red
pencil
12" x 10""
2001

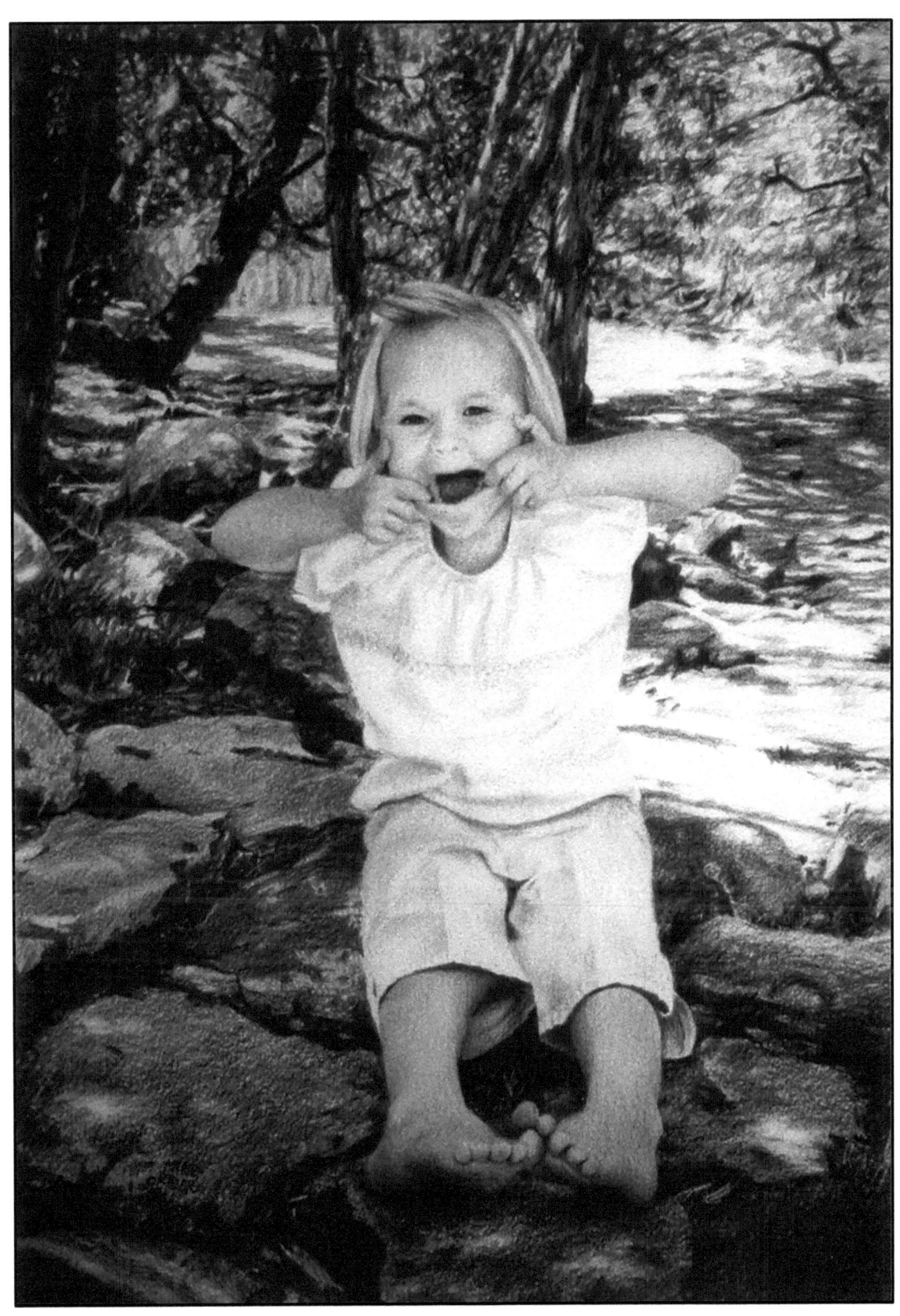

Harris
pencil
15" x 11"
2000

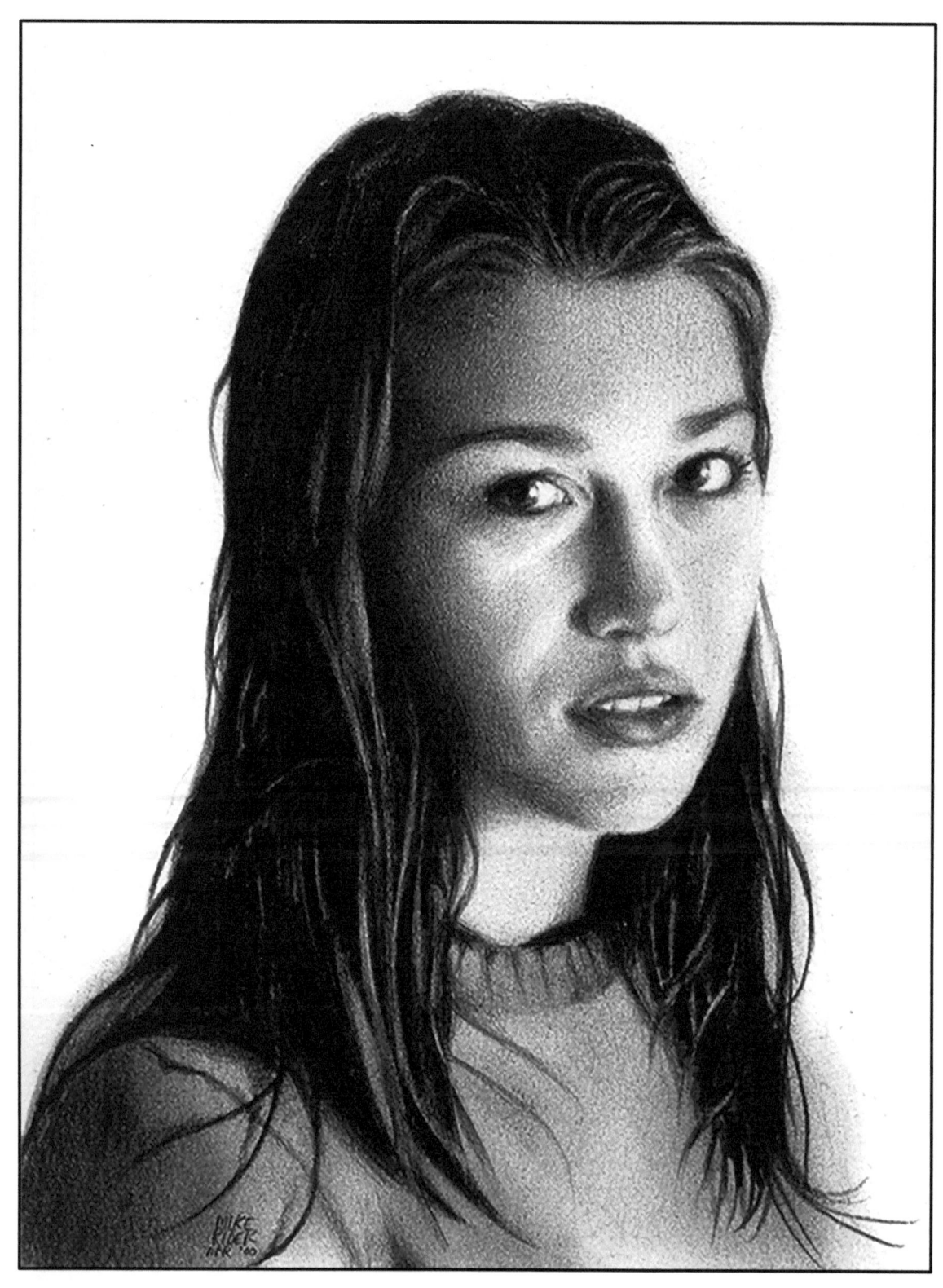

Jessica
pencil
13" x 10"
2000

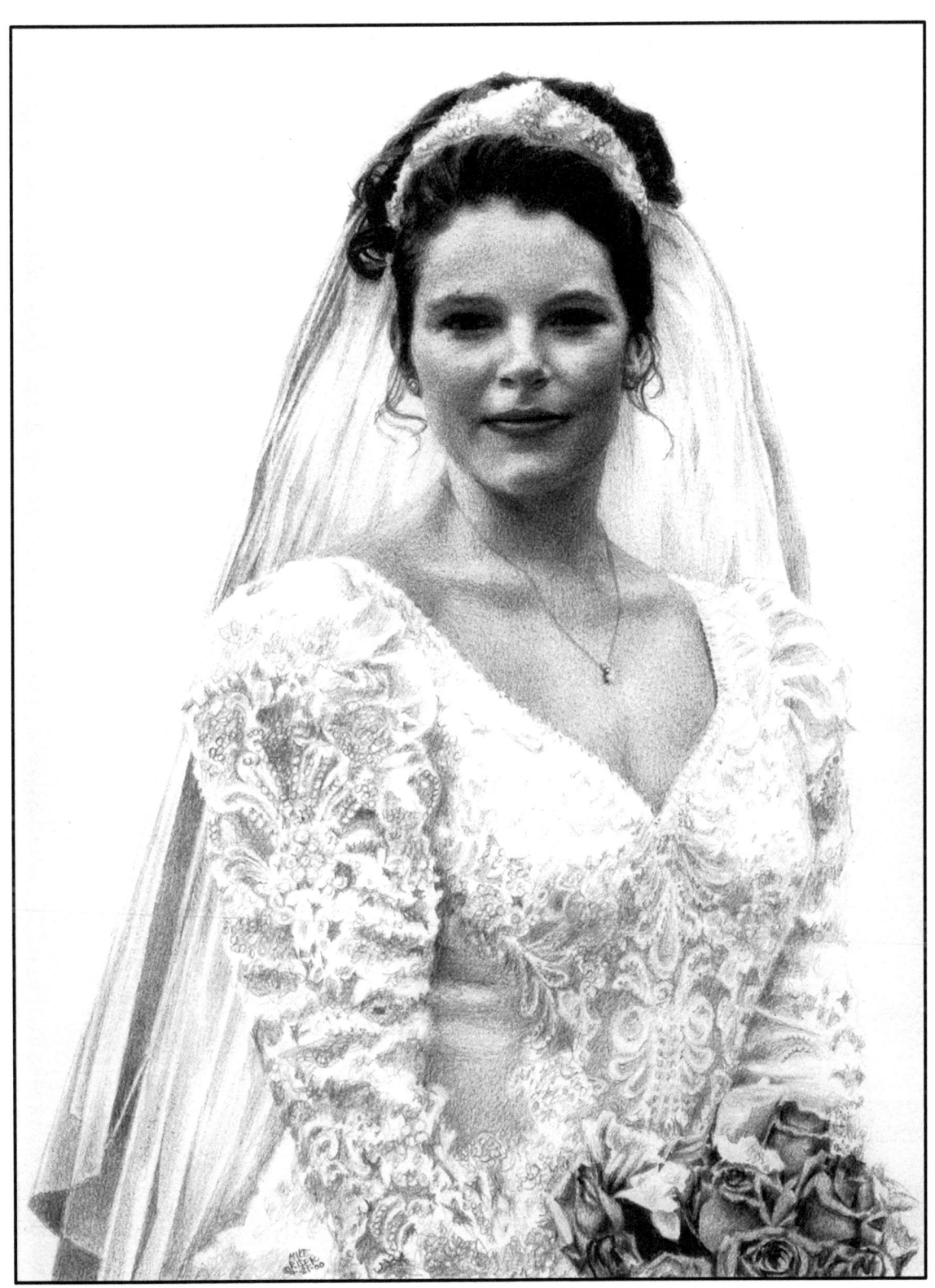

Wedding Day
pencil
12" x 10"
2000

13

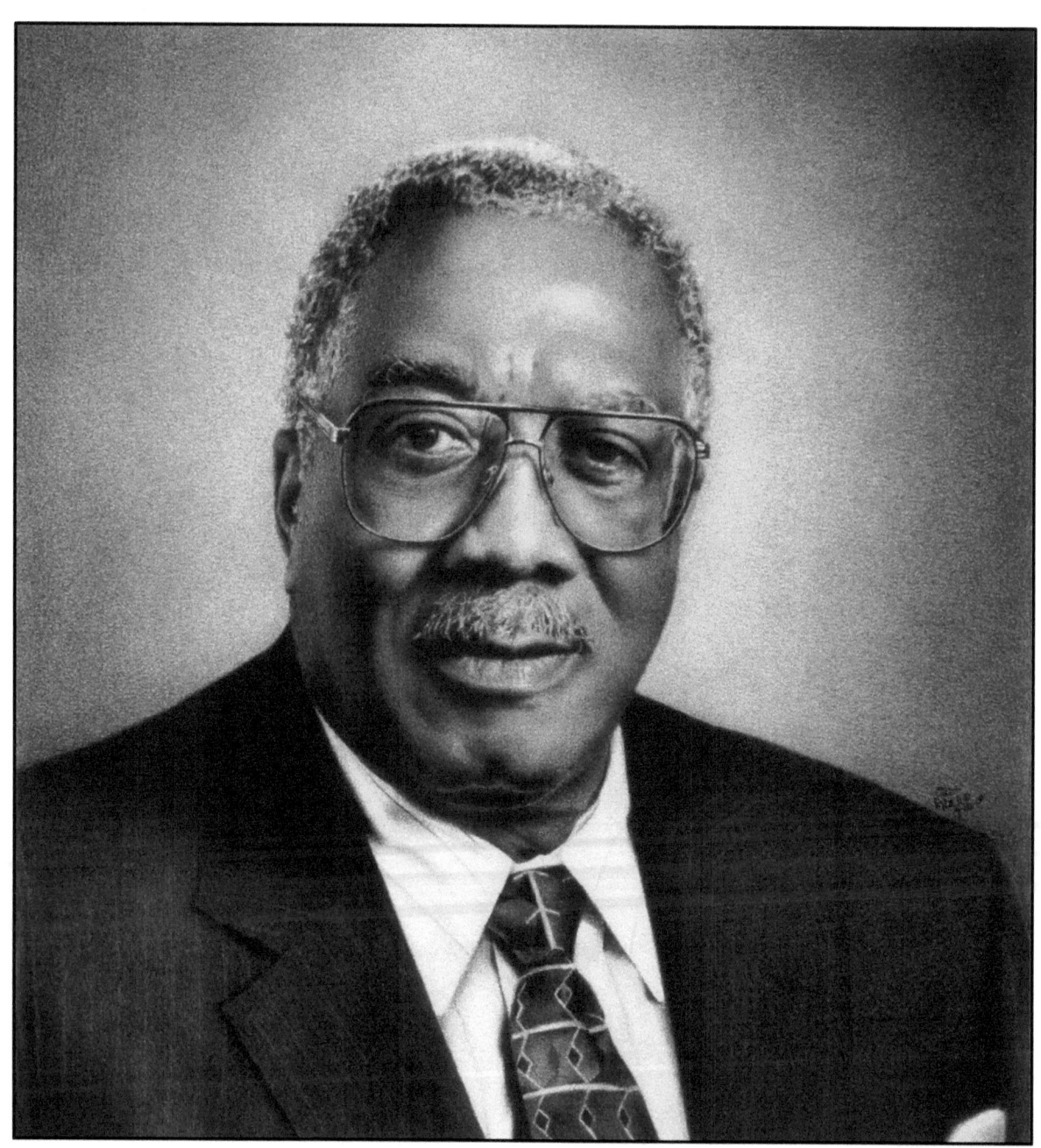

Joseph Brown
pencil
21" x 17"
2001

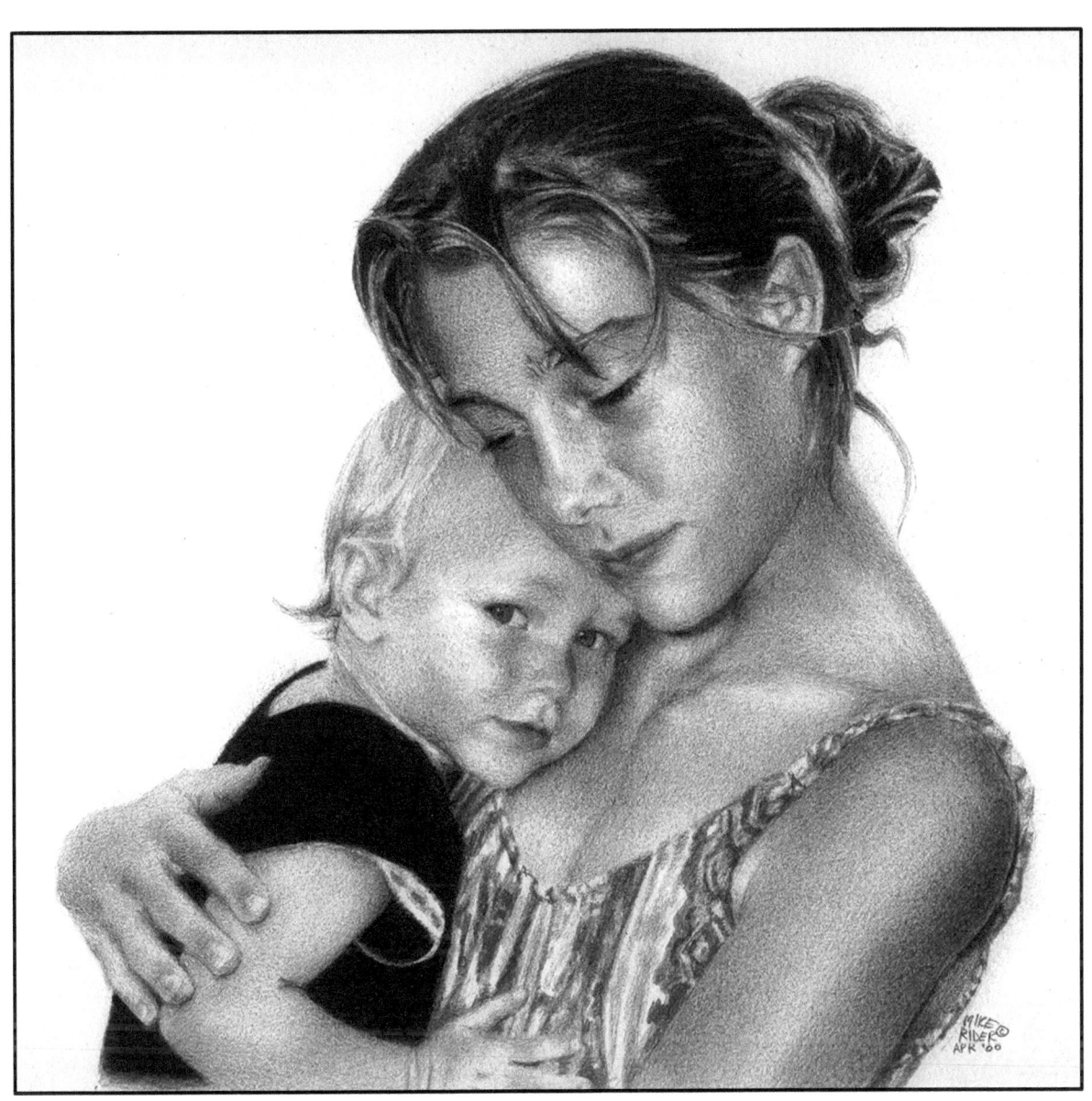

Sisters
pencil
10" x 12"
2000

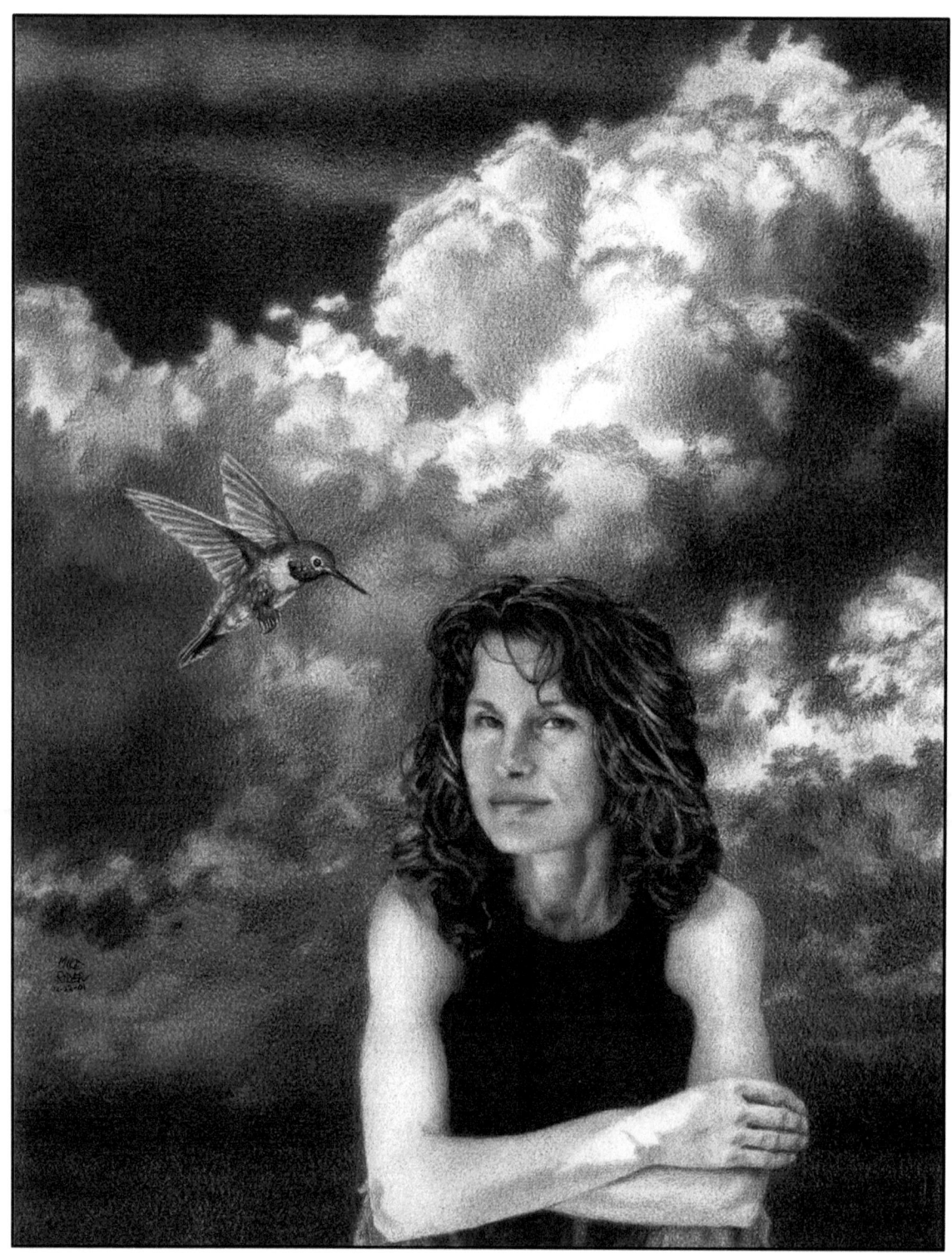

Sharon
pencil
13" x 11"
2001

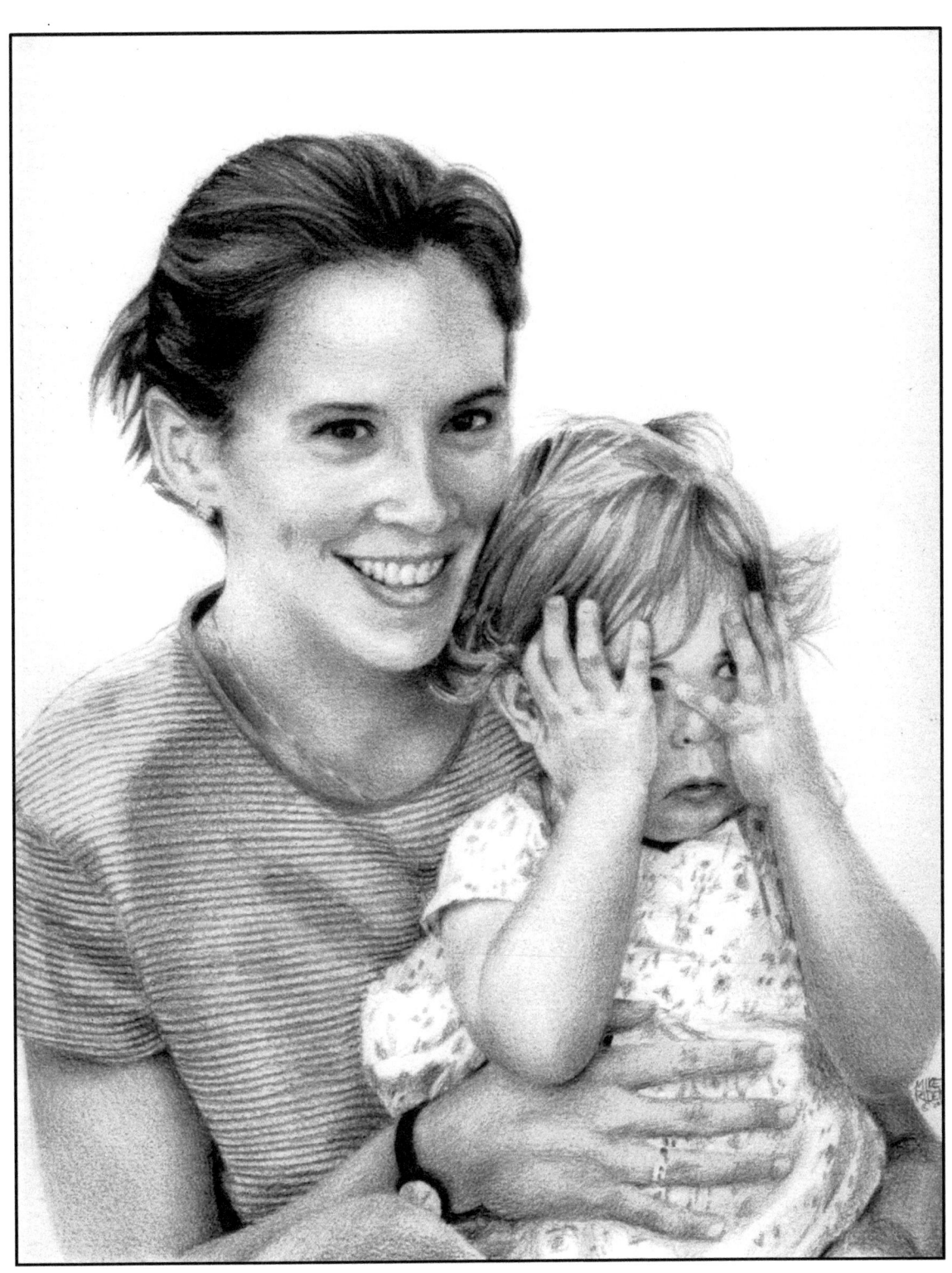

Kelly and Claire
pencil
12" x 10"
2001

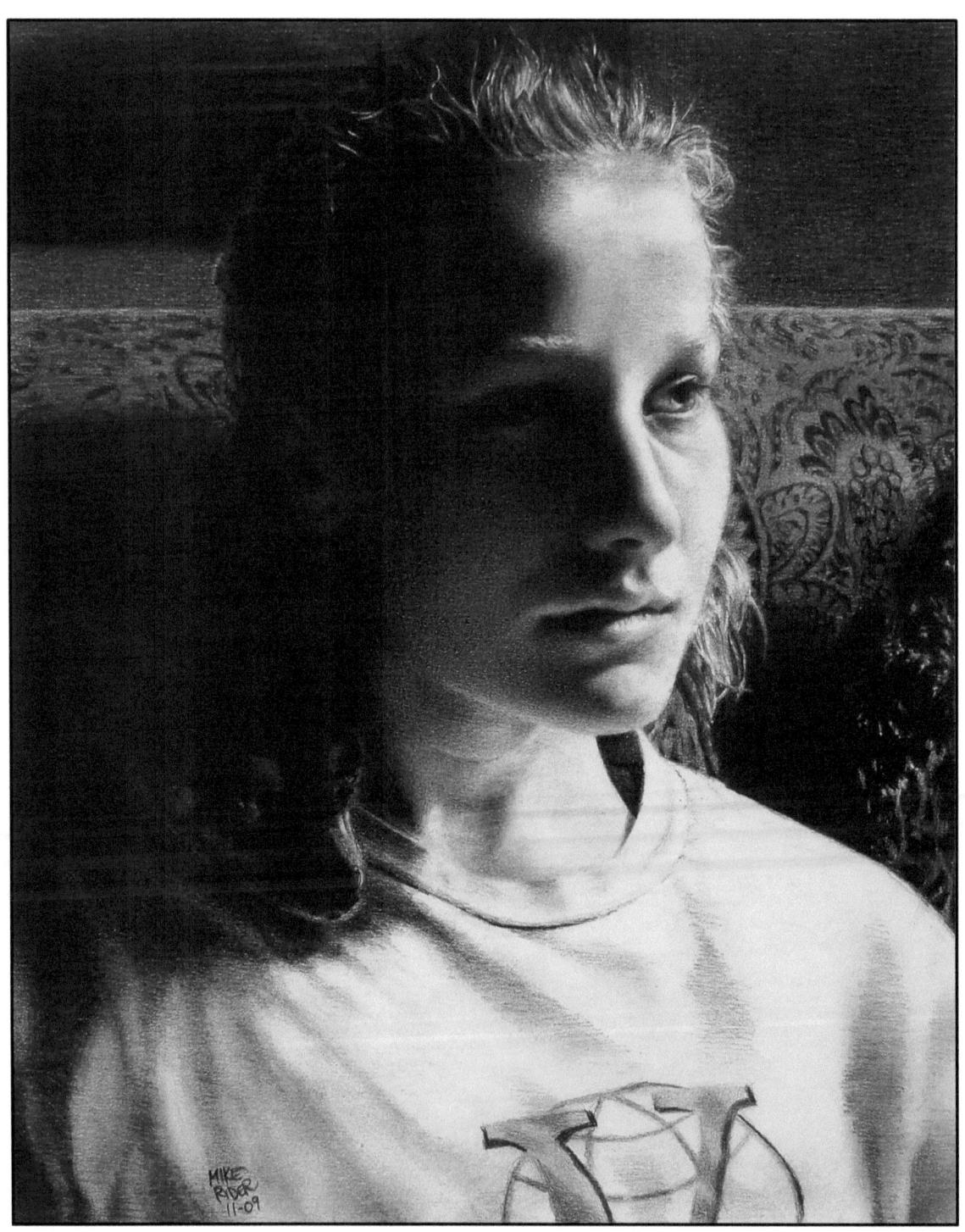

Sixteen
pencil
12" x 10"
2009

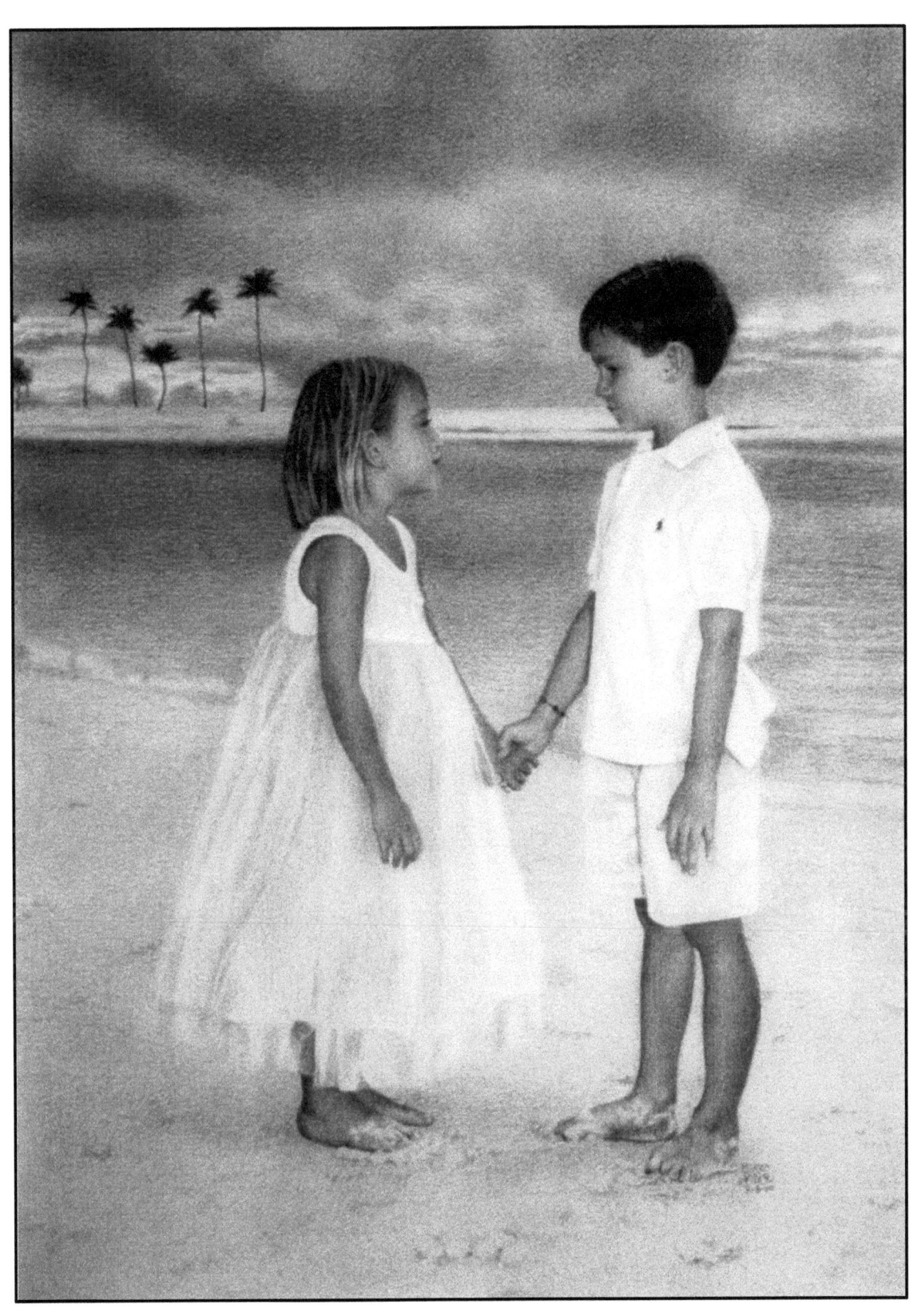

Mason and Andrew
pencil
15" x 11"
2000

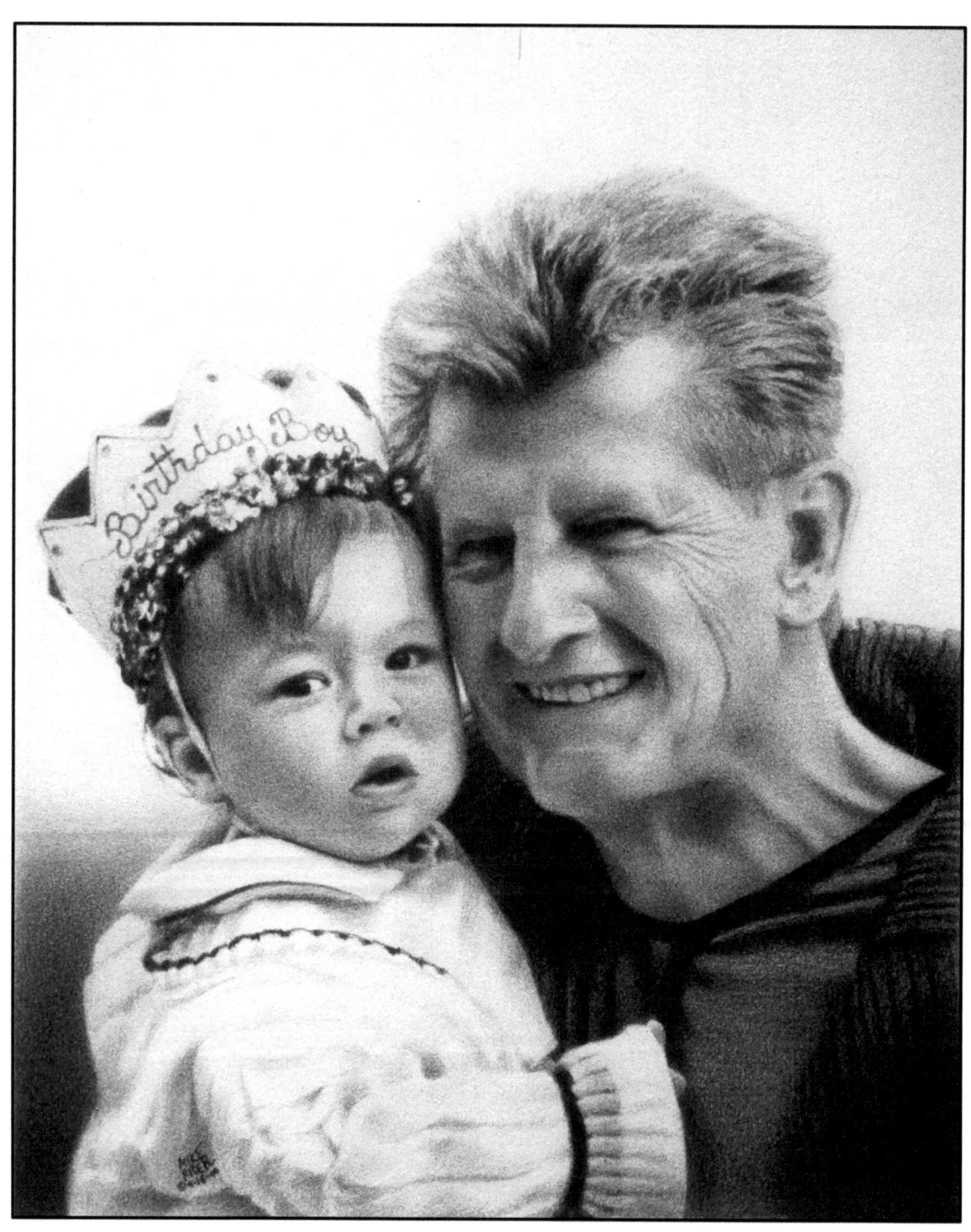

Grandfather and Grandson
pencil
13" x 11"
2000

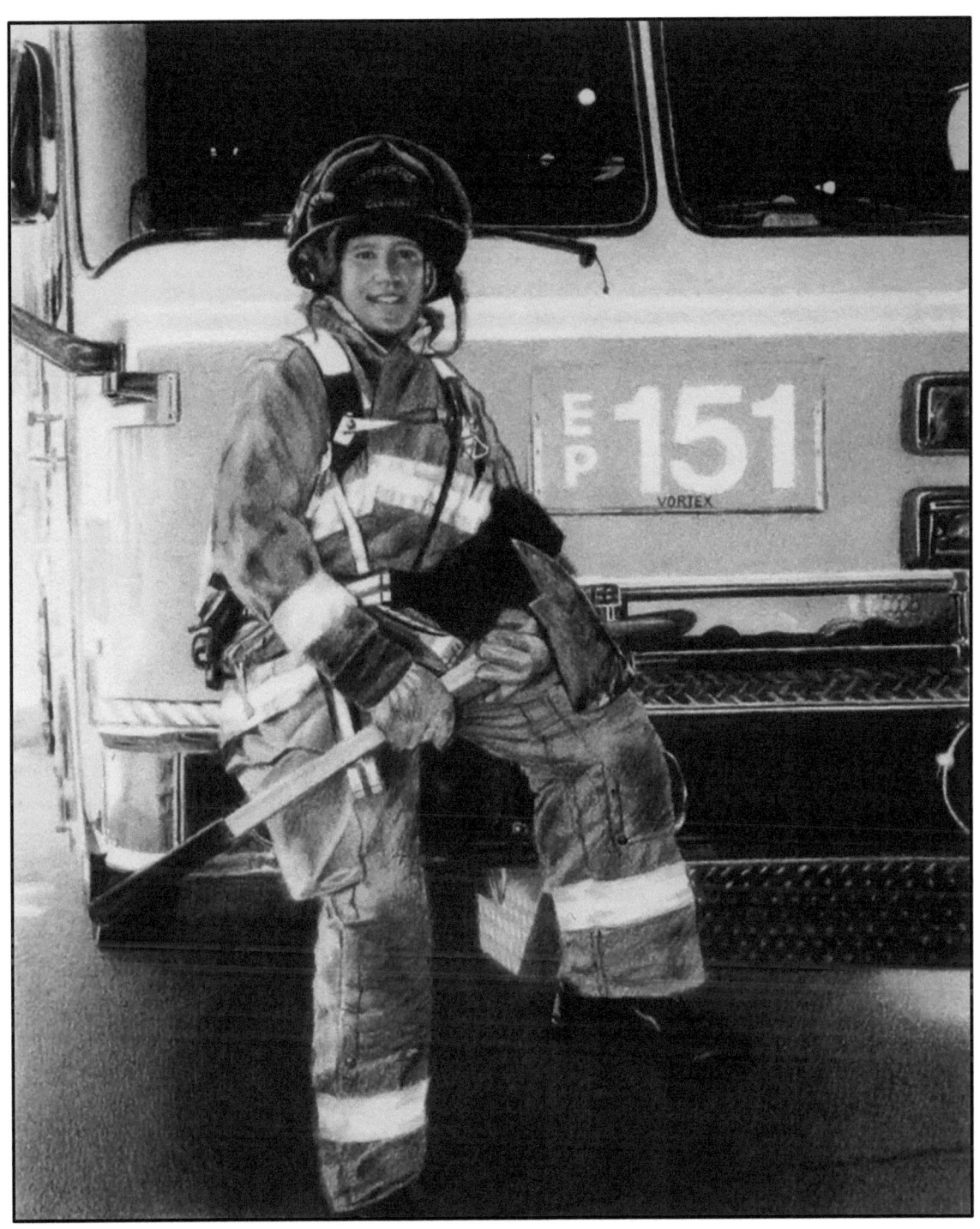

Linda
pencil
13" x 11"
2000

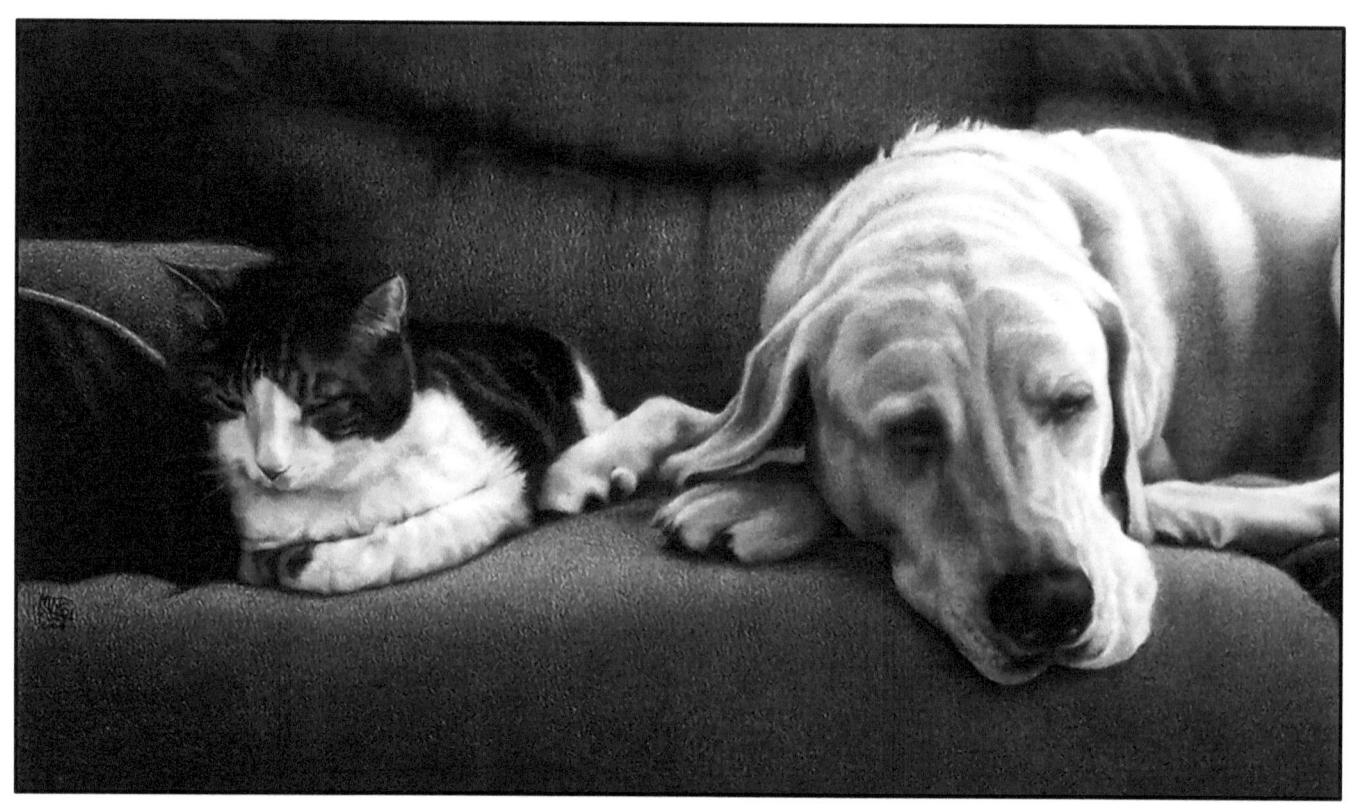

Above:
Break Time
pencil
13" x 22.5"
2008

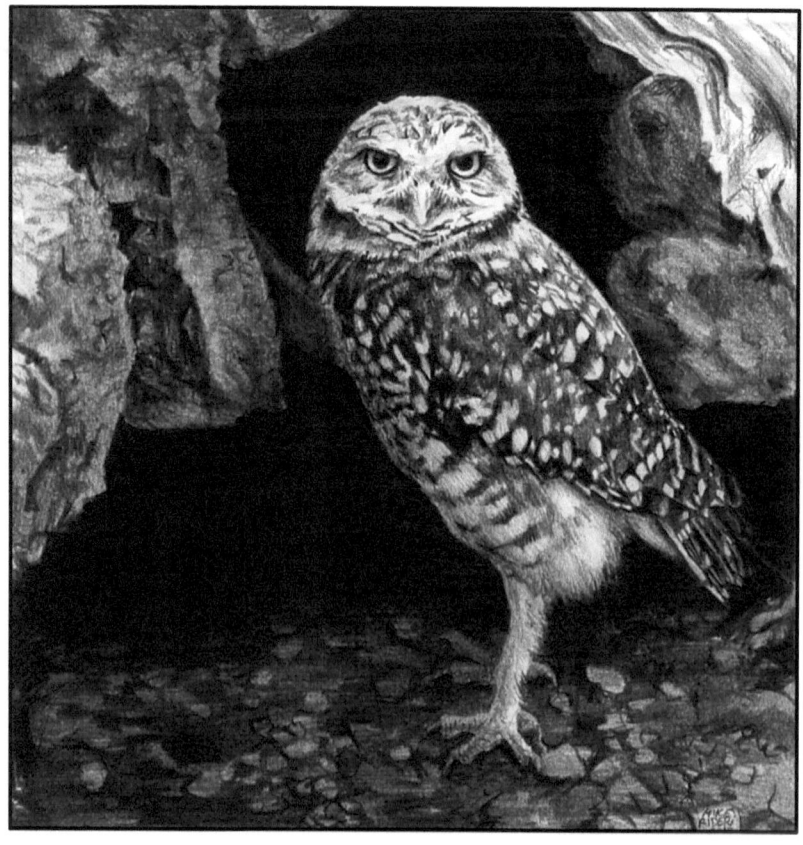

Left:
Burrowing Owl
pencil
6" x 6"
2010

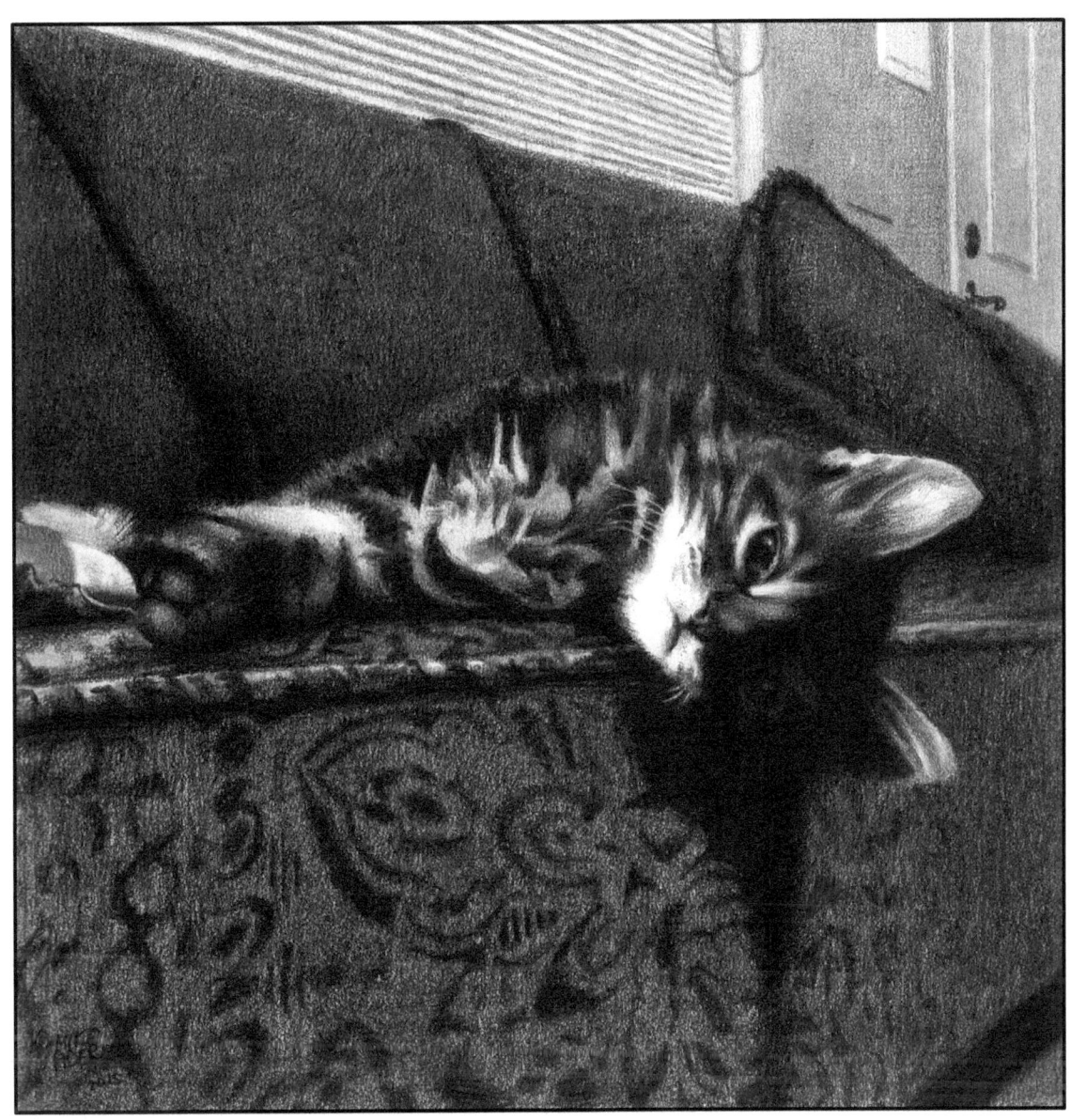

Hypnosis
pencil
8" x 8"
2015

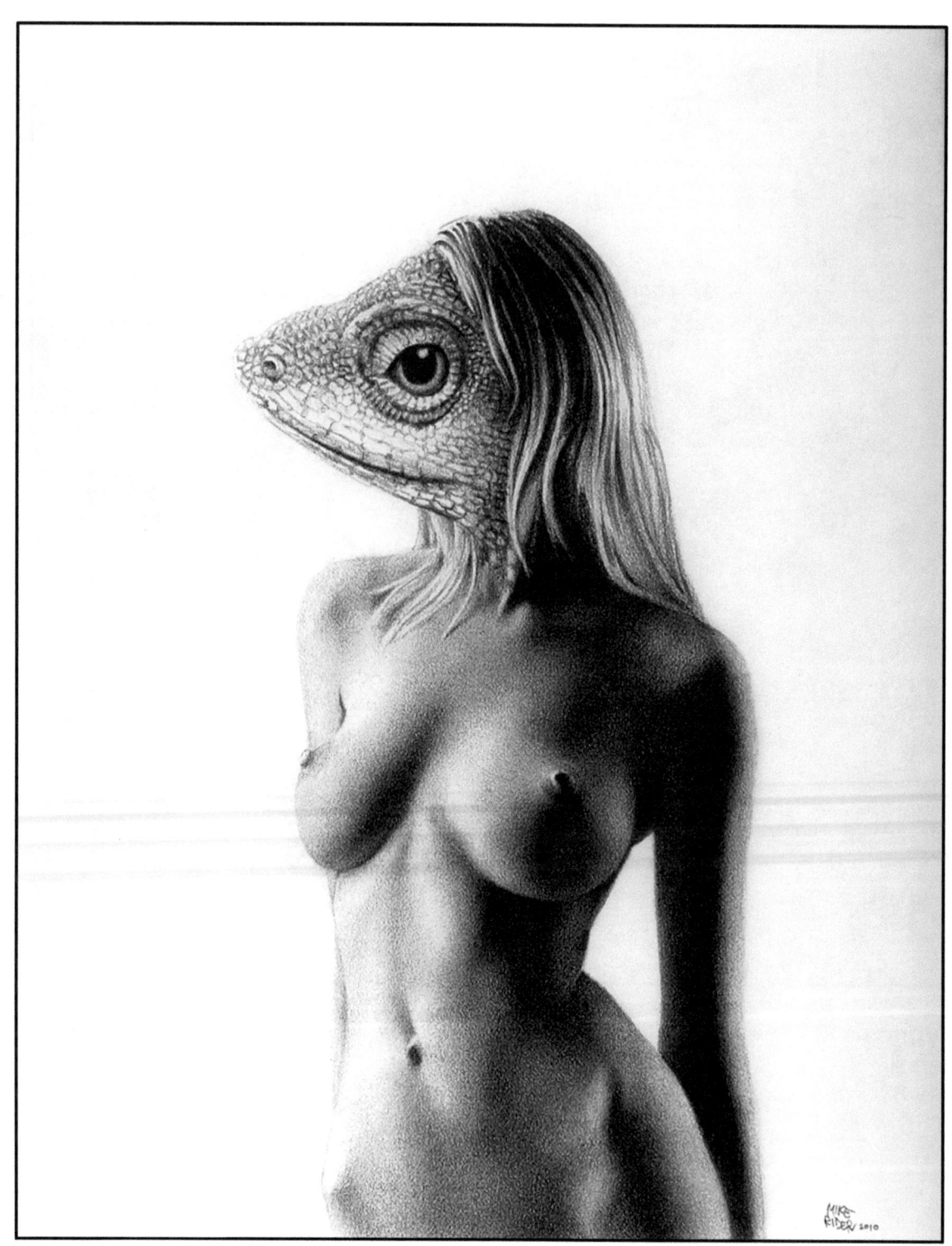

Until…
pencil
10" x 8"
2010

Paintings

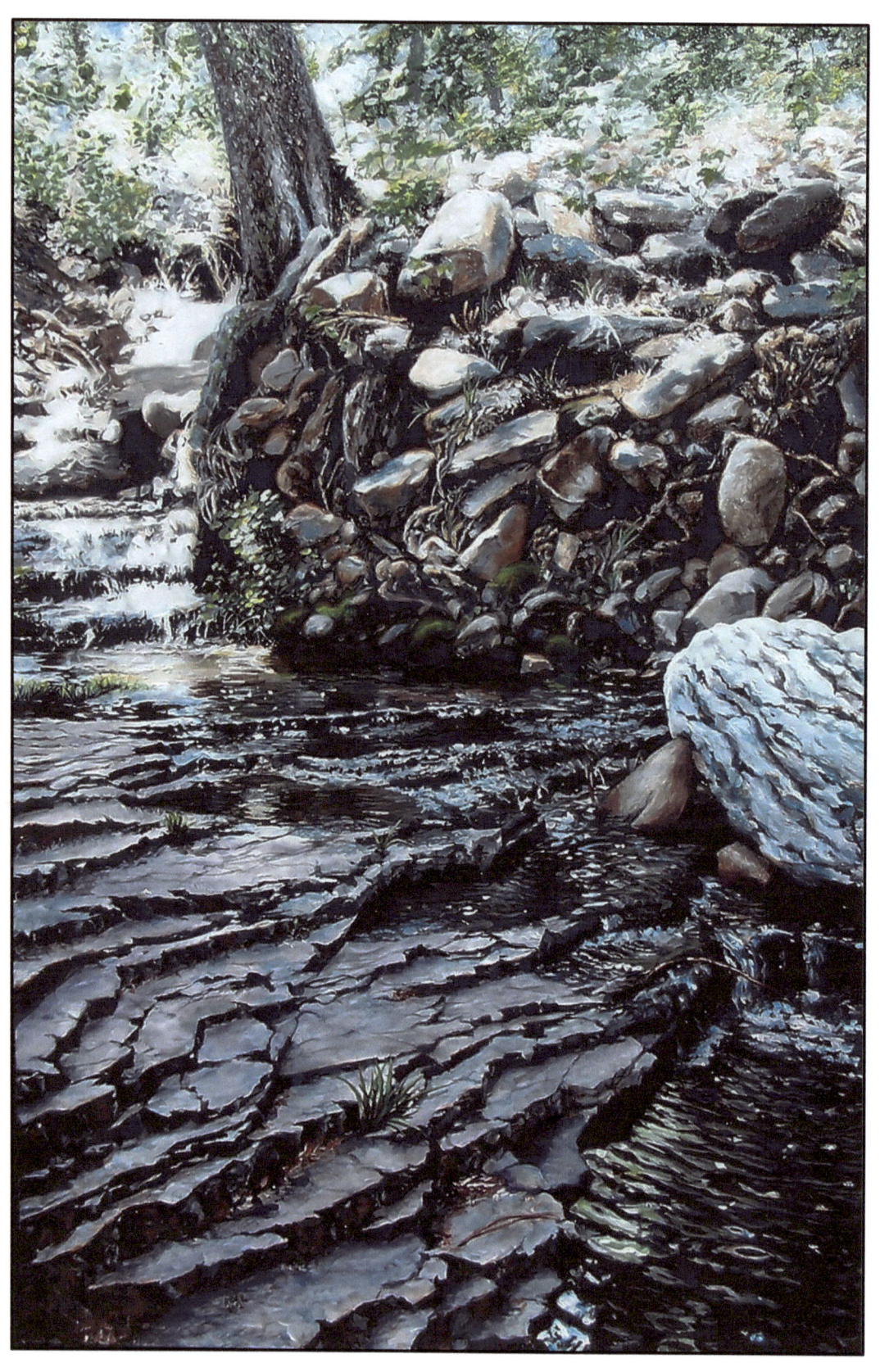

Workman Creek
acrylic on canvas
26" x 24"
2005

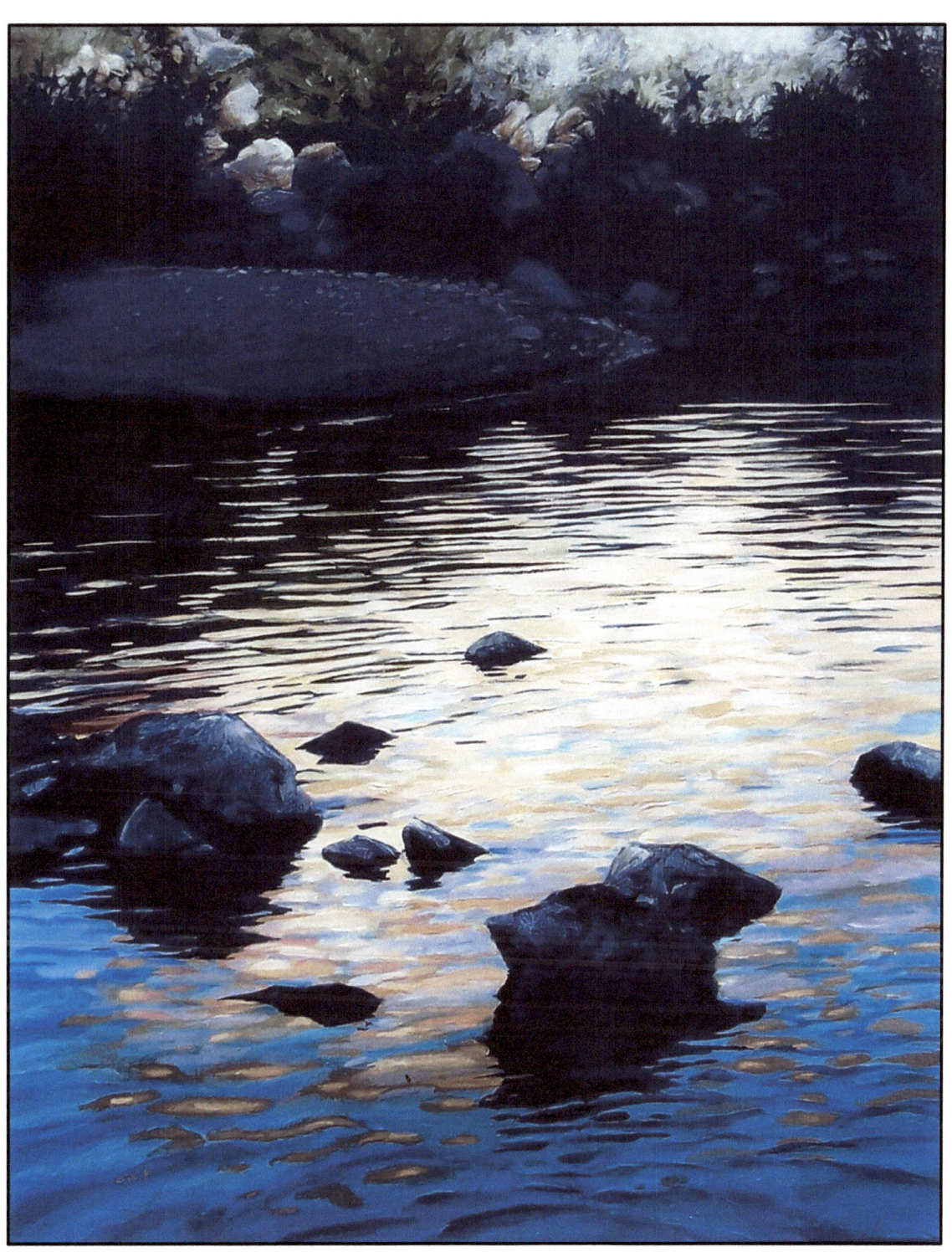

Tortilla Creek
acrylic on canvas
20" x 16"
2006

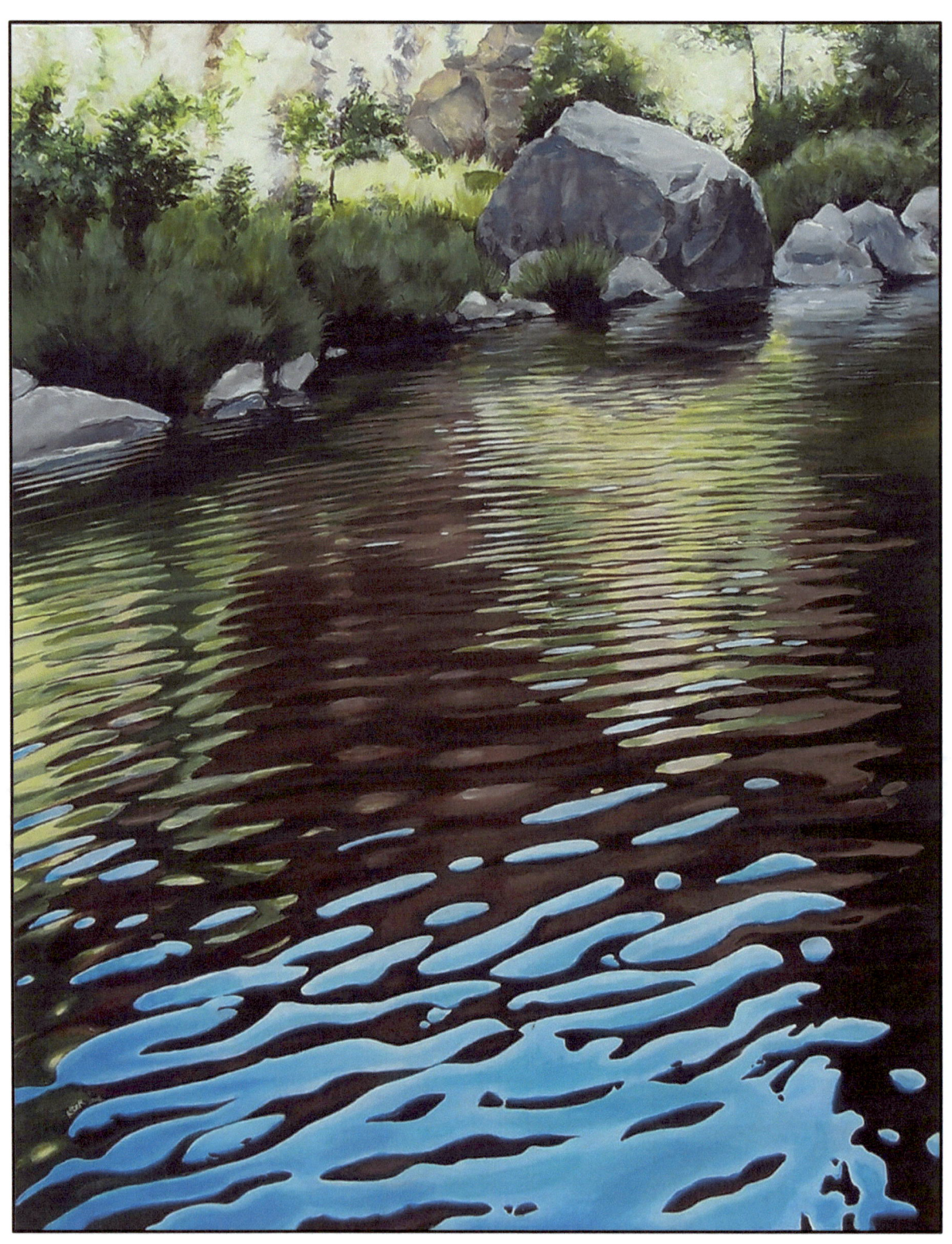

West Clear Creek
acrylic on canvas
30" x 24"
2006

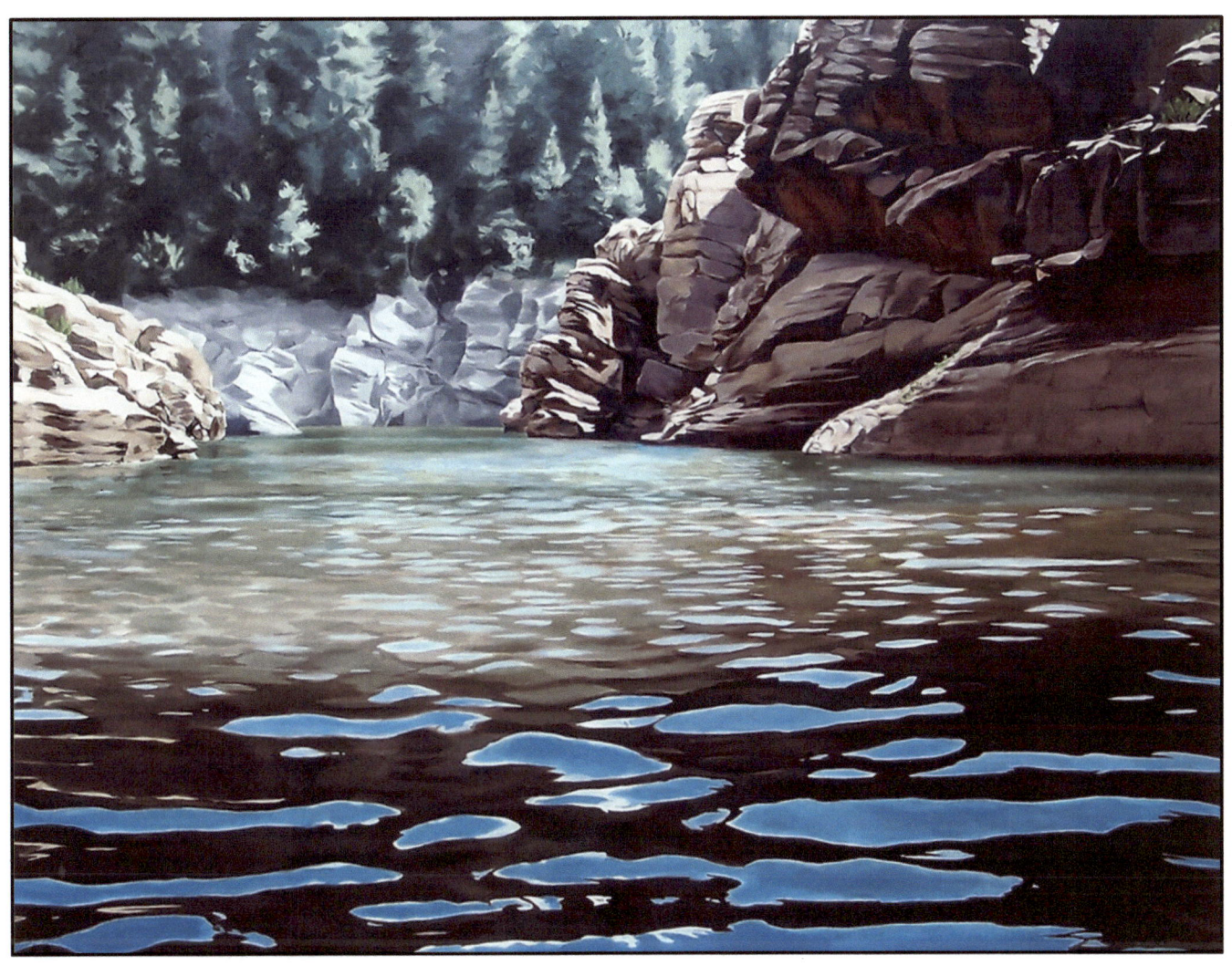

Blue Ridge
oil on canvas
30" x 40"
2007

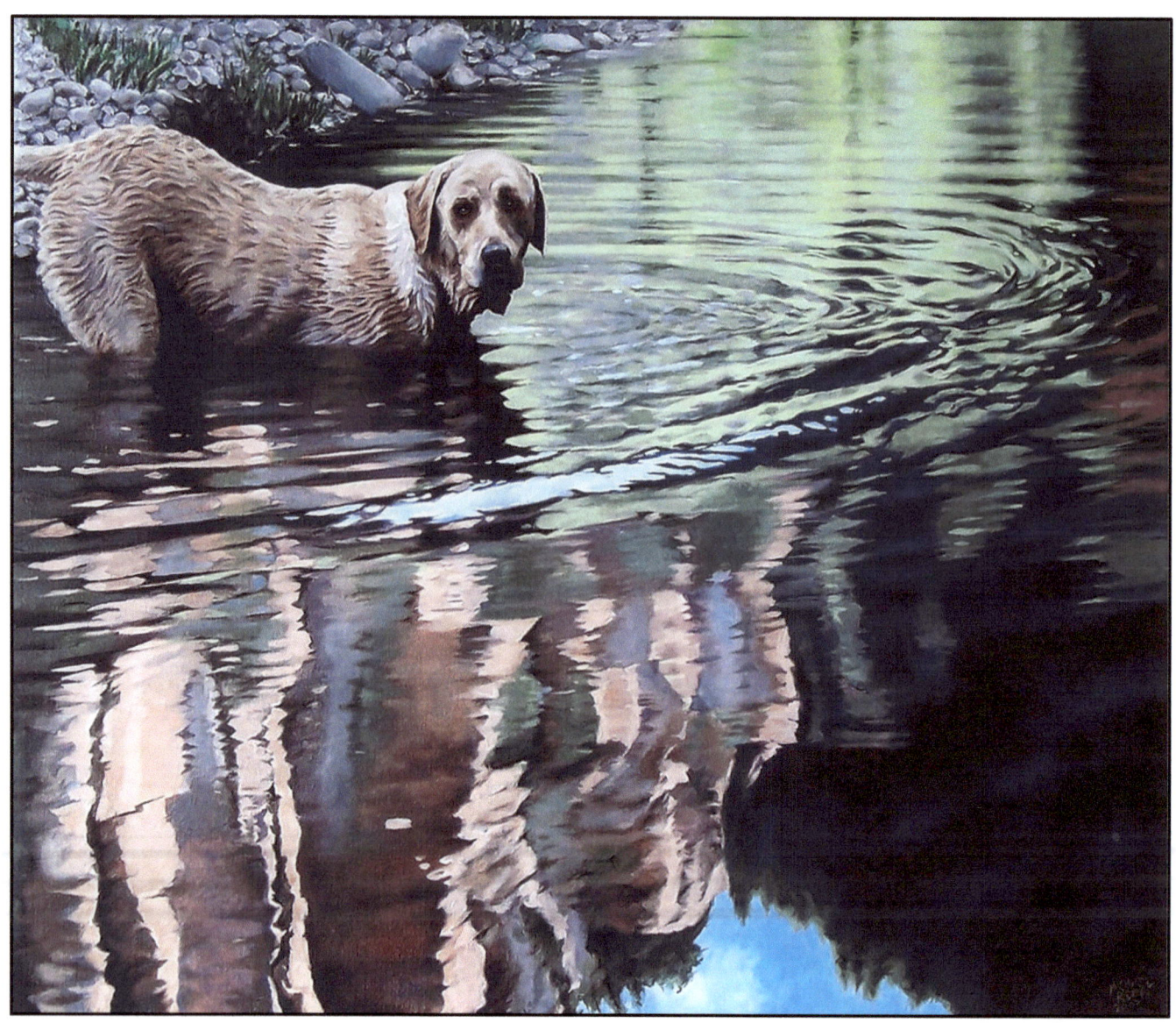

King Snake Canyon
oil on canvas
20" x 24"
2007

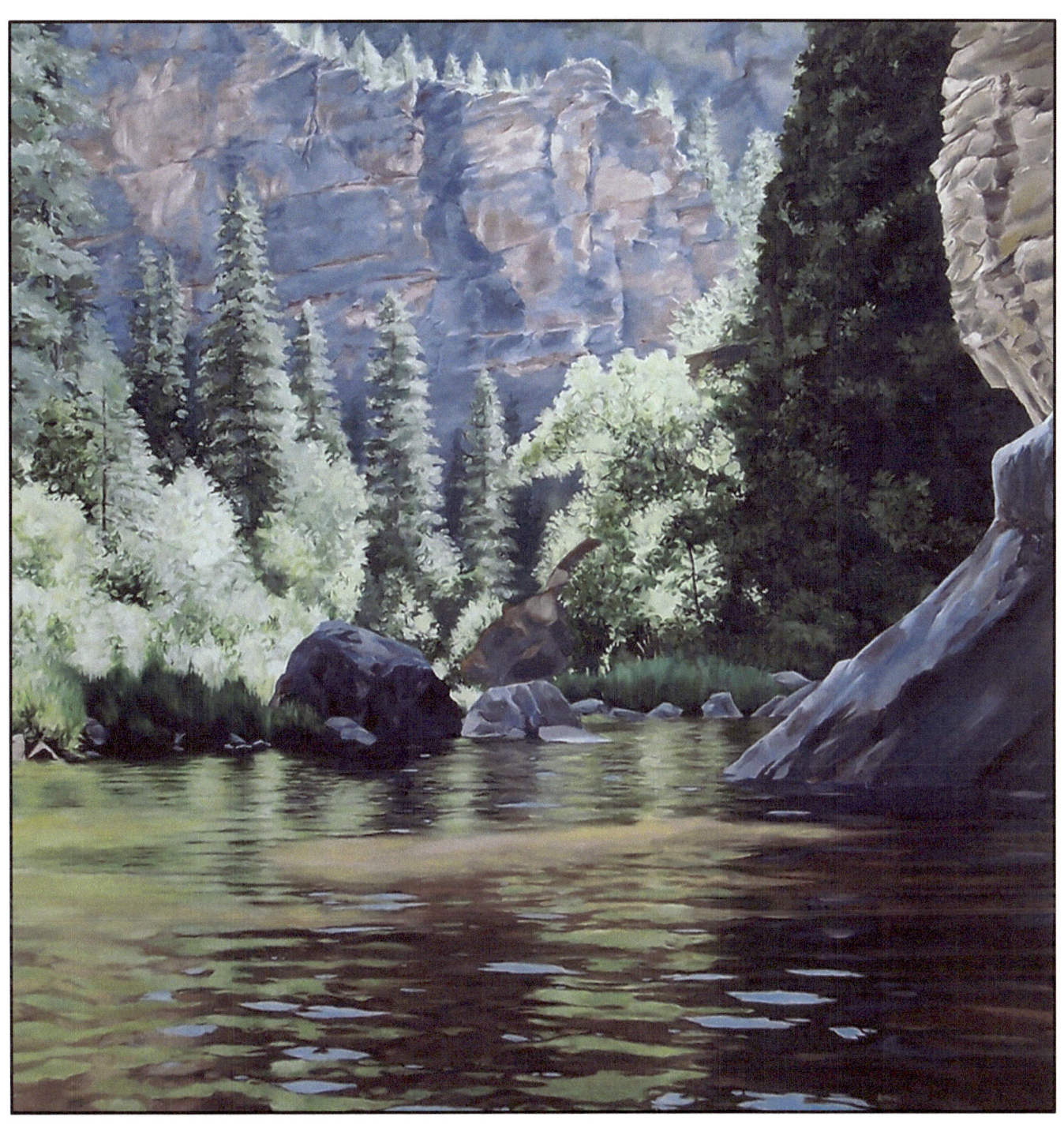

Windy Canyon Creek
oil on canvas
26" x 36"
2007

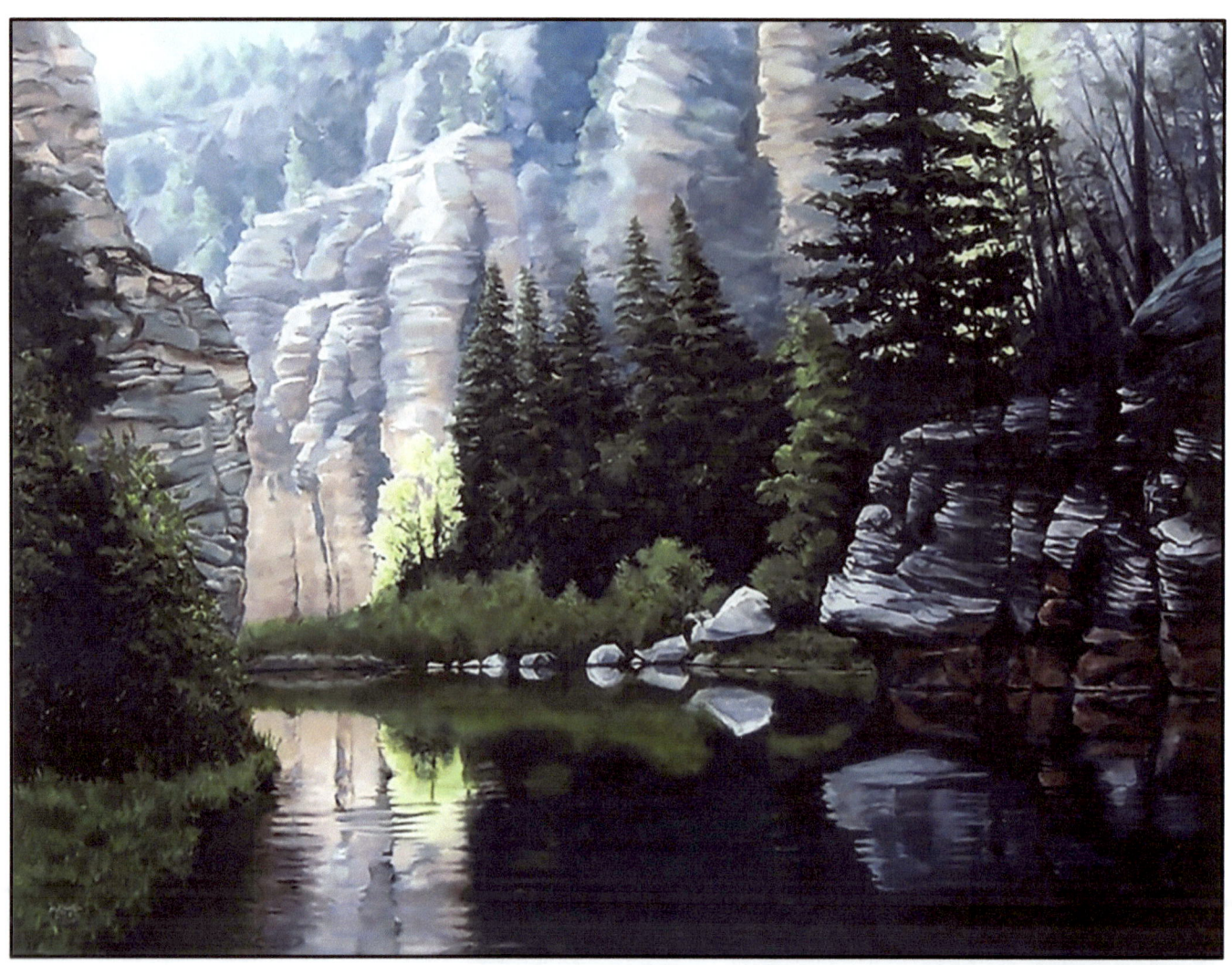

Sanctuary
oil on canvas
30" x 40"
2008

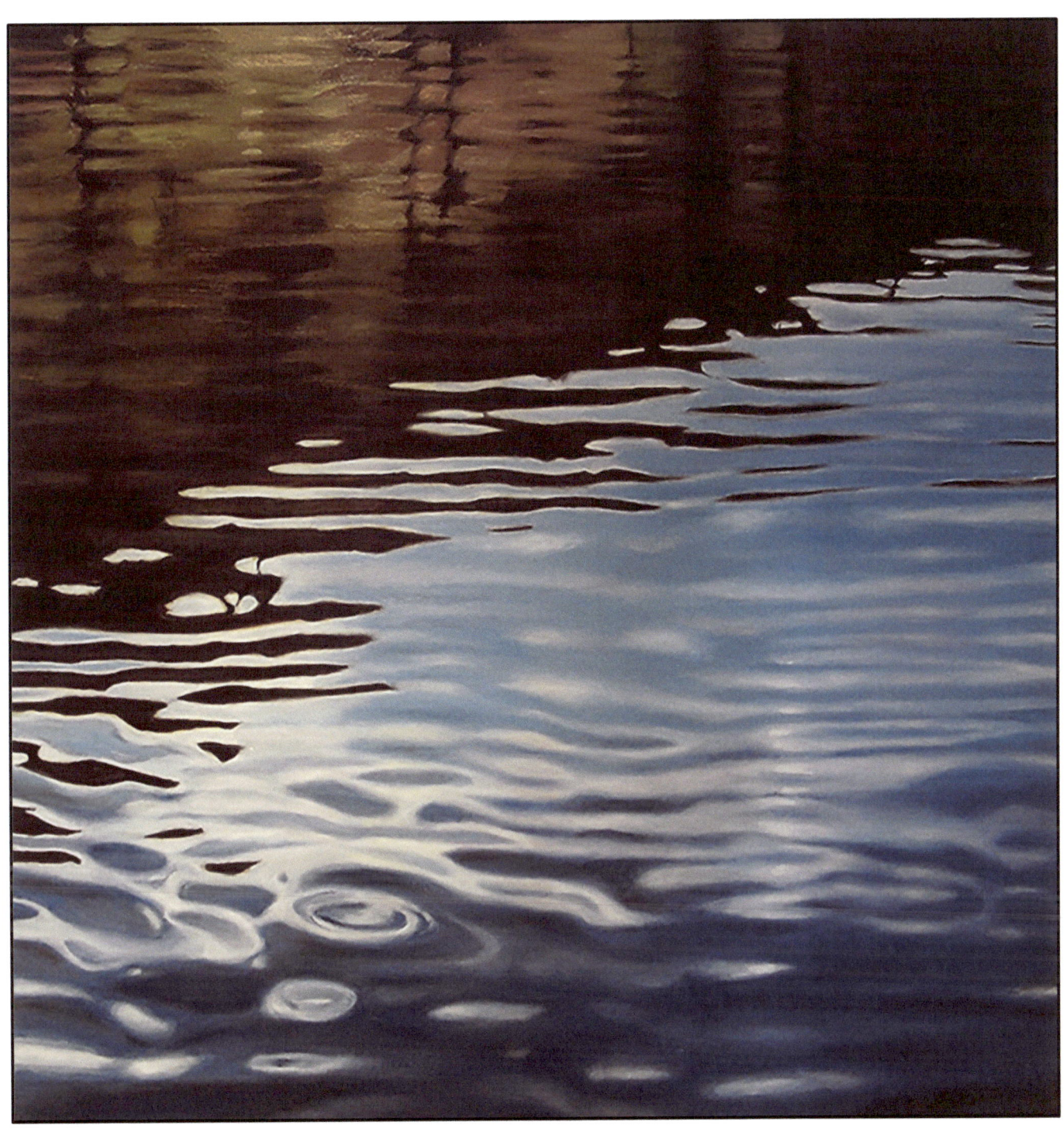

The Veil
oil on canvas
30" x 30"
2009

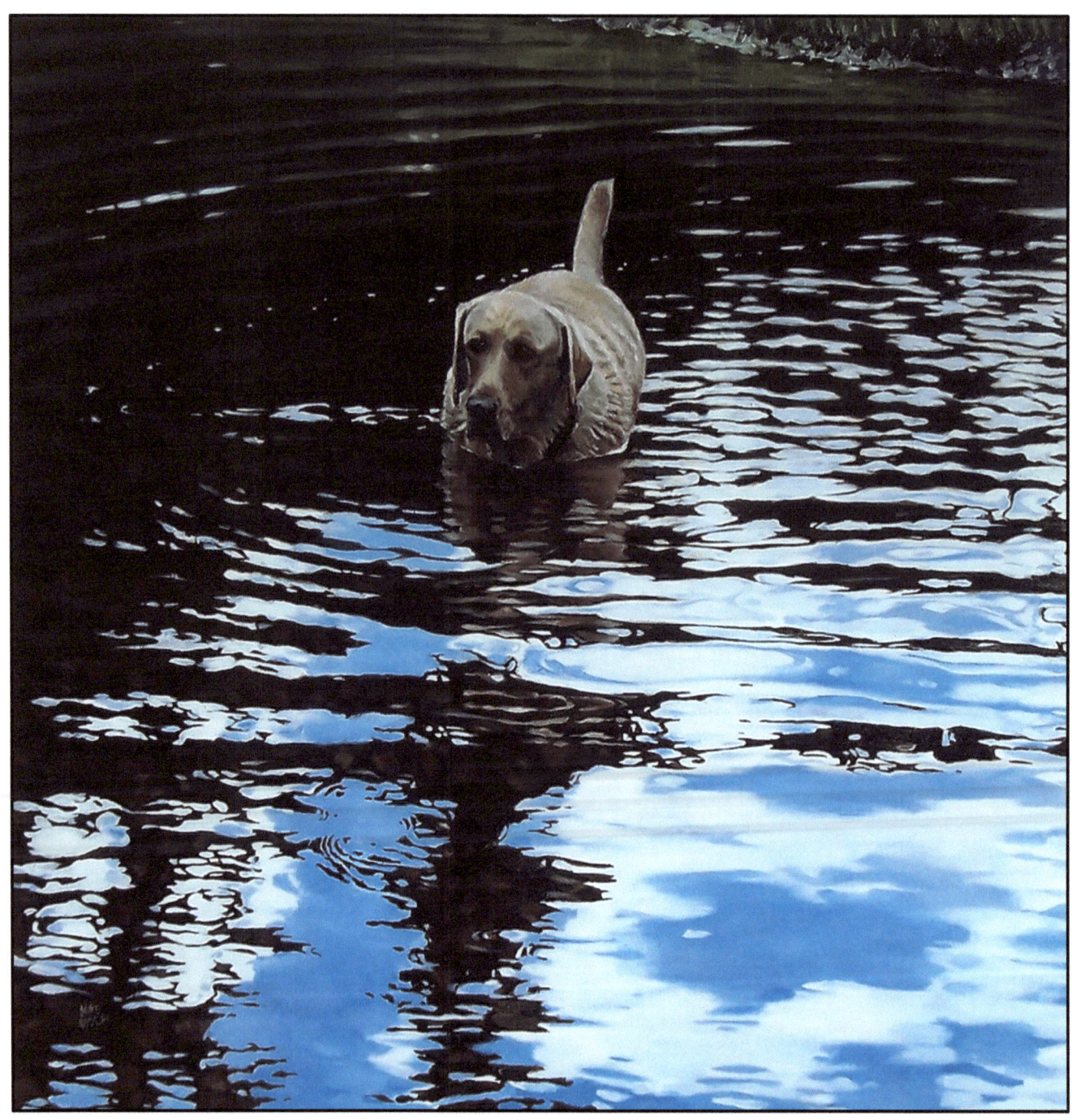

No Hurry
oil on canvas
24" x 24"
2009

Opposite page:
Where the Elk Roam *(top)*
oil on board
9" x 12"
2013

Walking Back *(bottom)*
oil on board
9" x 12"
2013

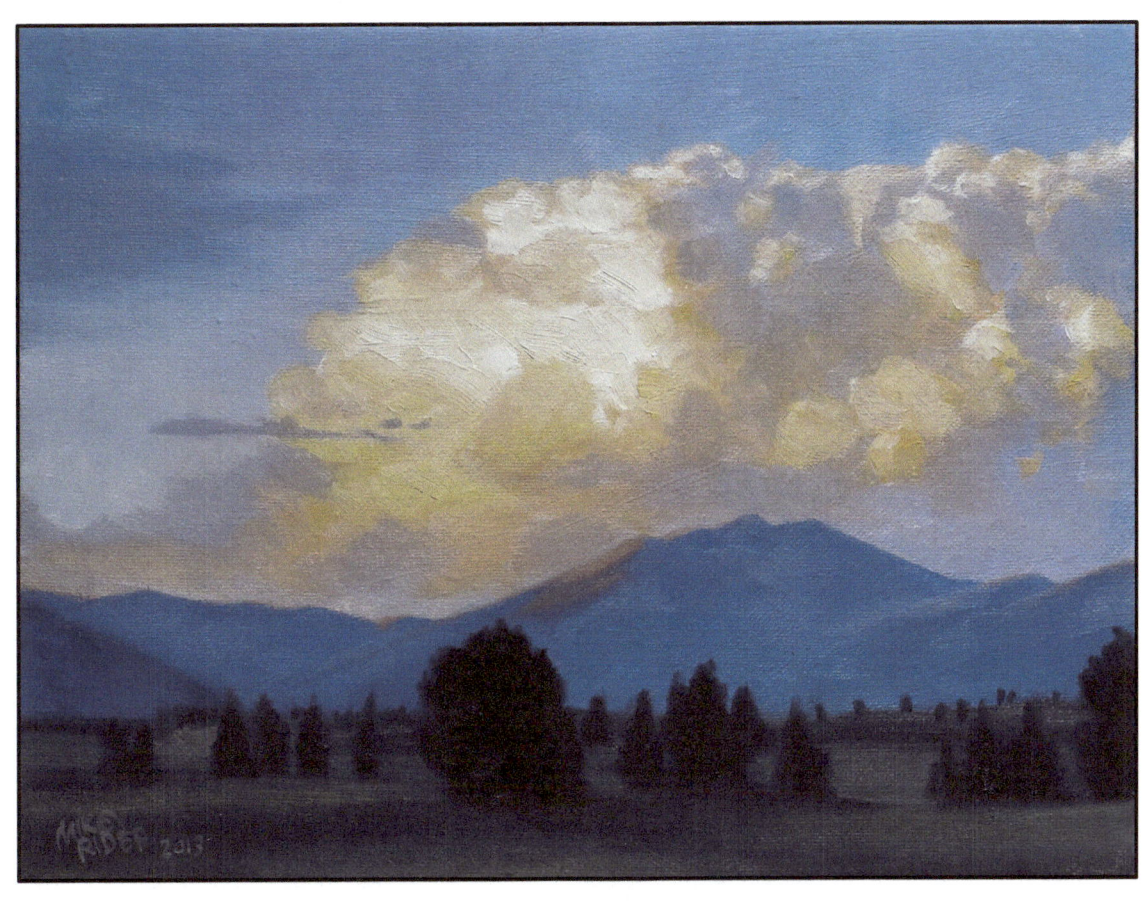

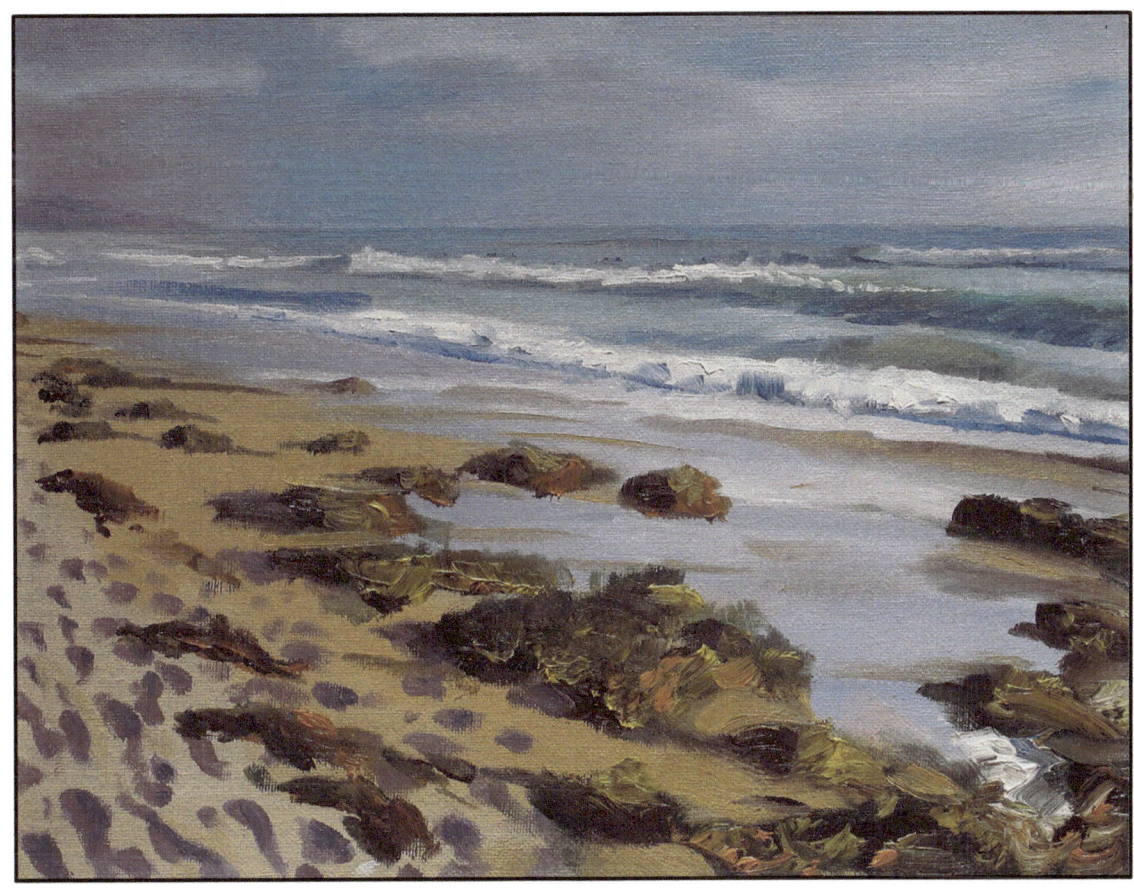

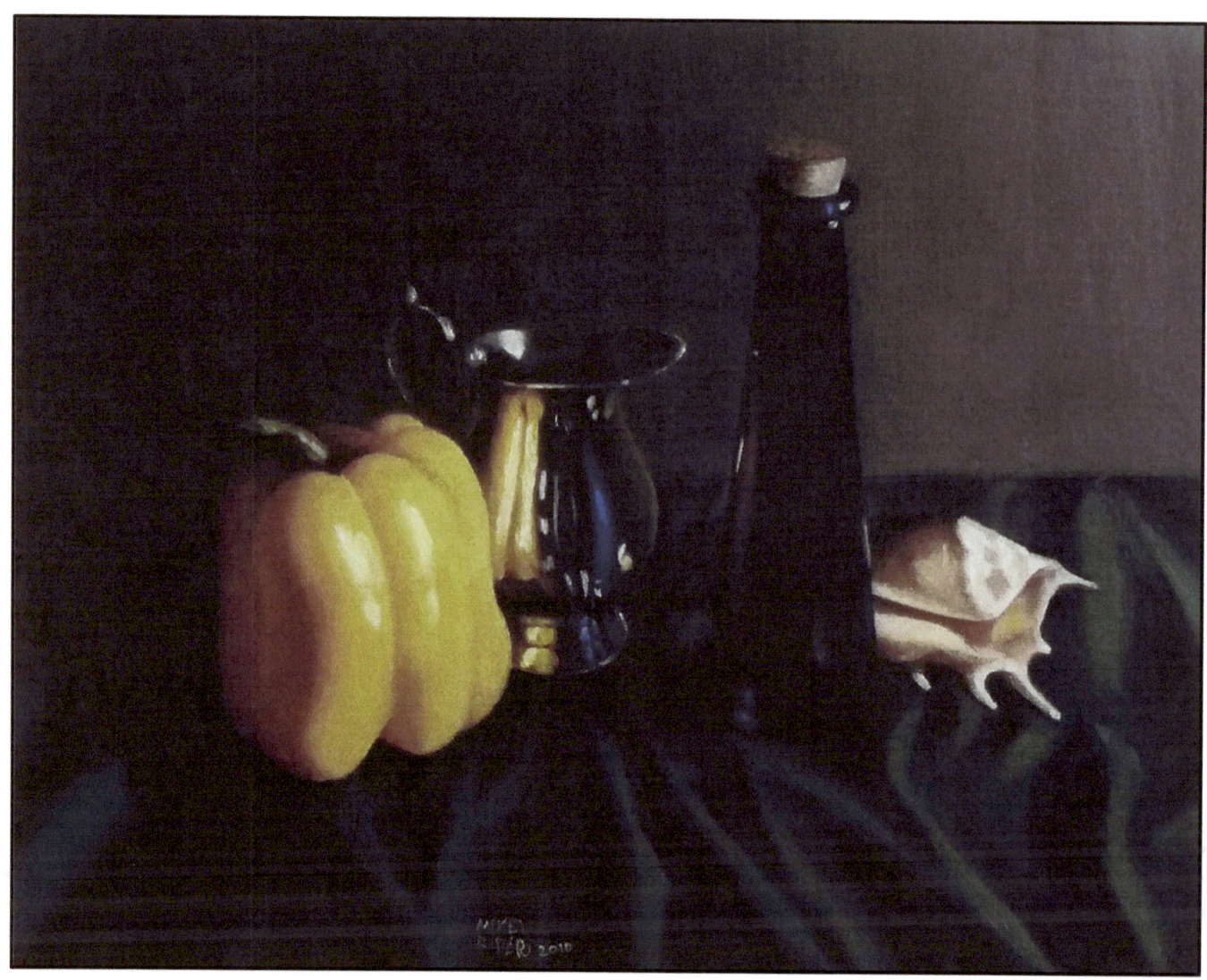

Alchemy Suspect
oil on board
11" x 14"
2010

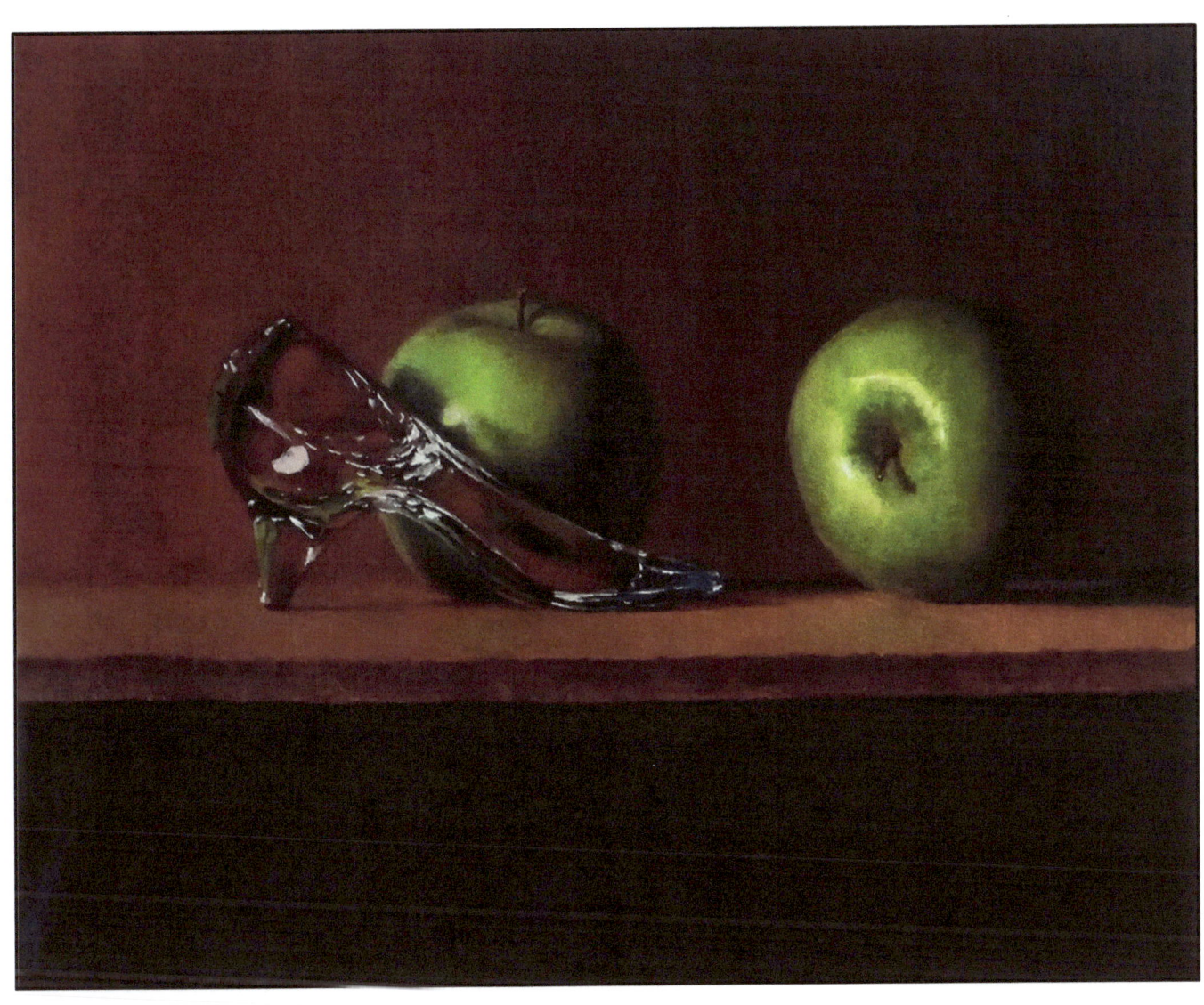

Tempted by Eileen
oil on board
11" x 14"
2010

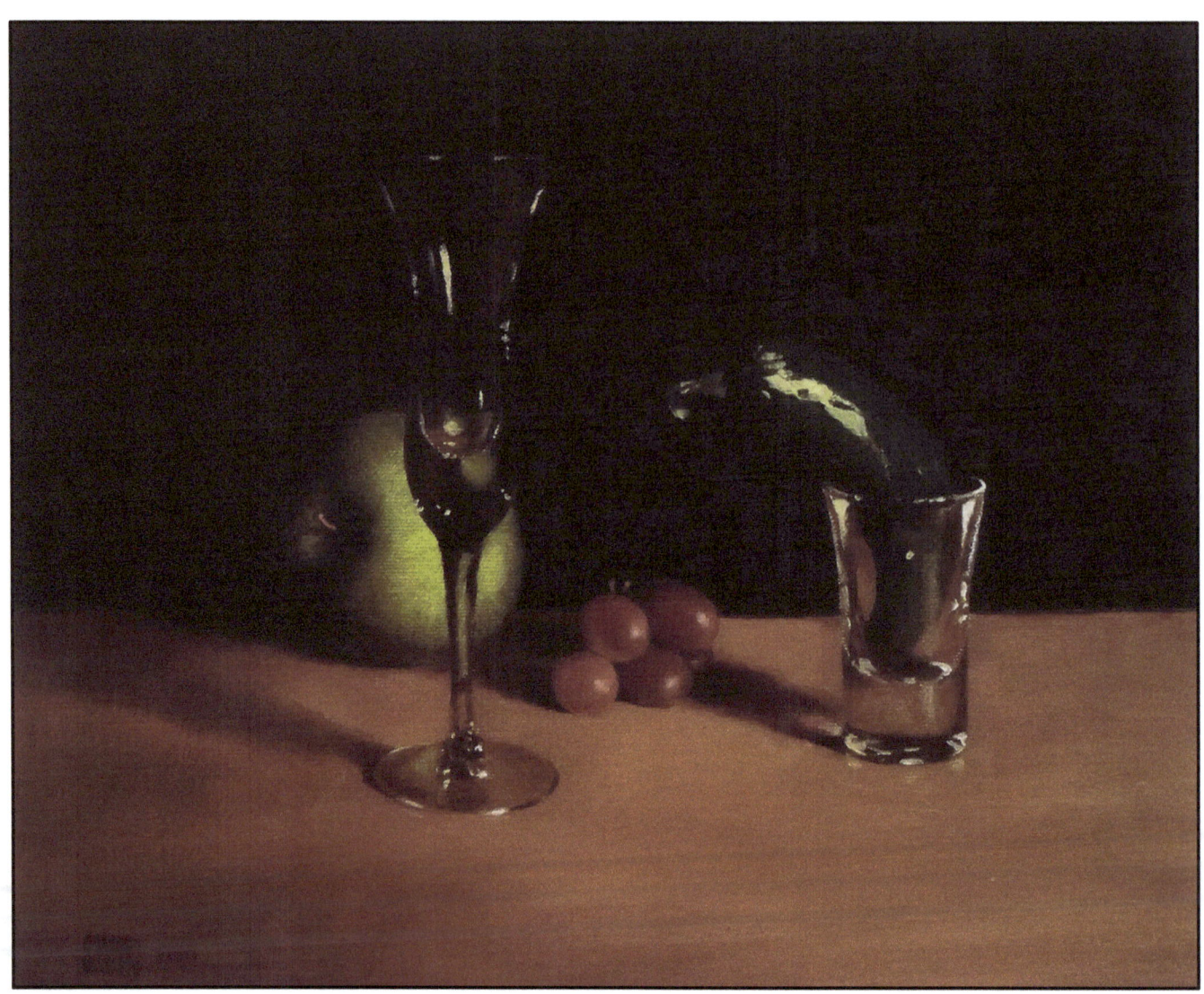

Fresh Start
oil on board
11" x 14"
2010

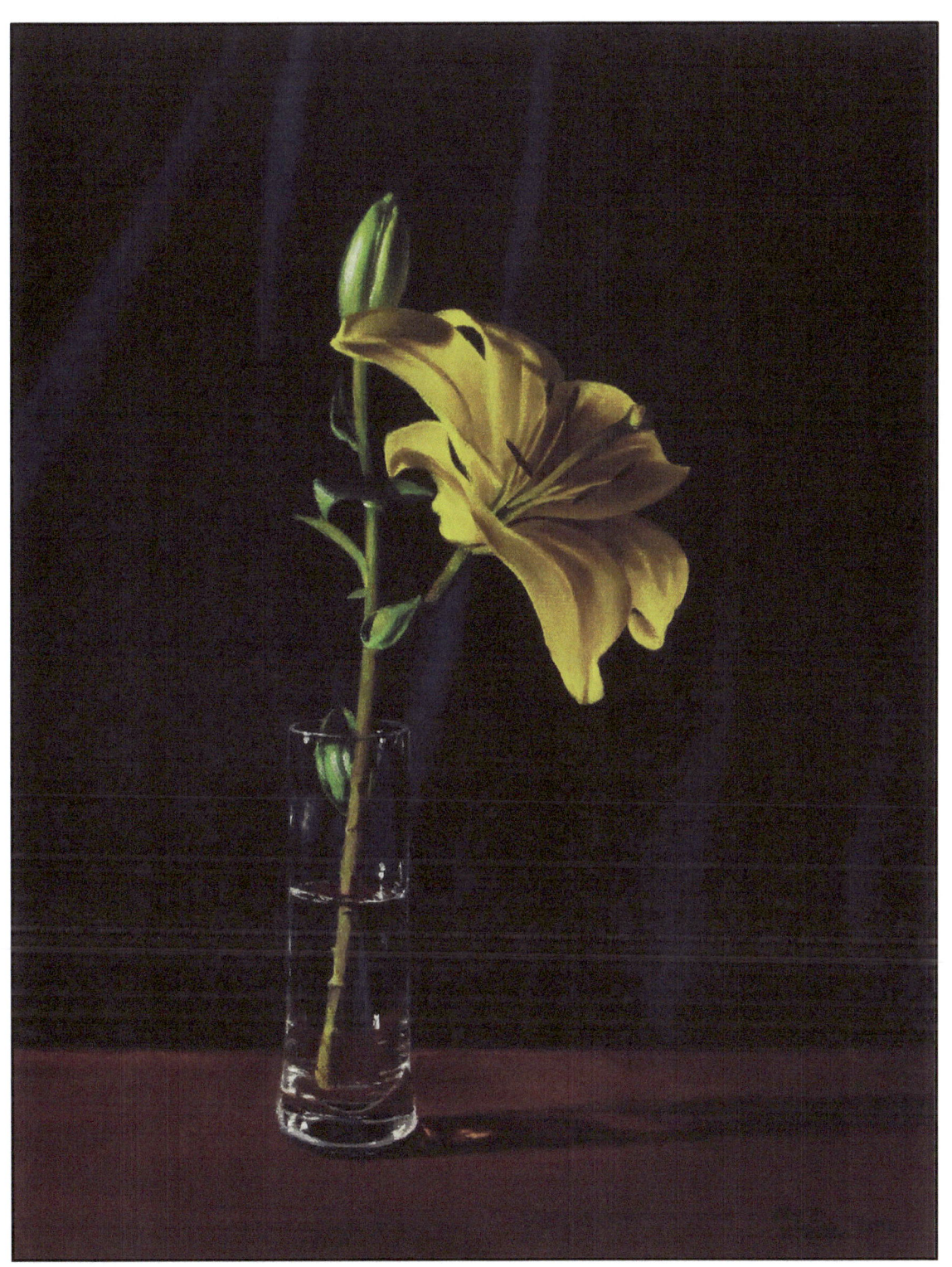

Solitary
oil on board
16" x 12"
2012

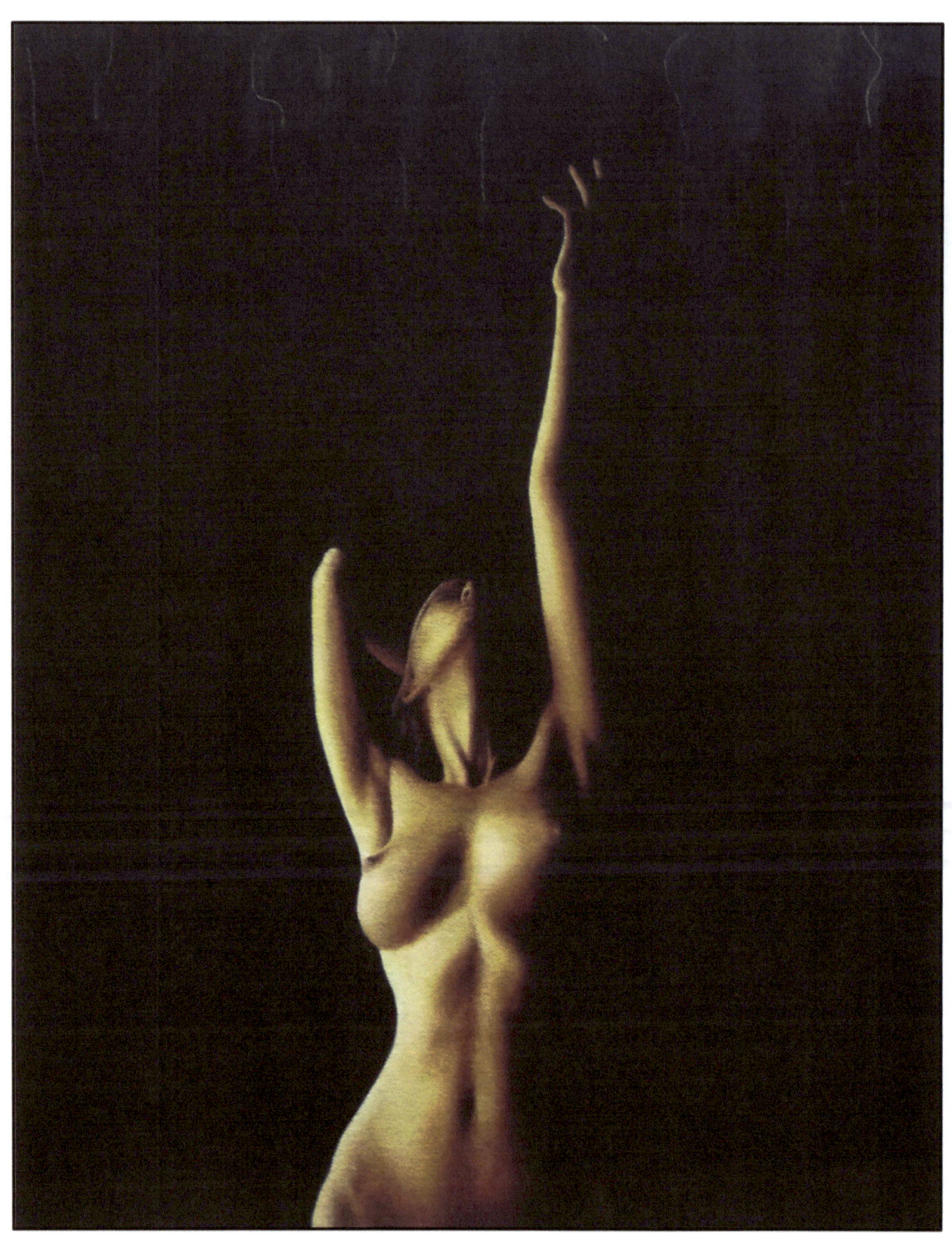

Almost There
oil on canvas
20" x 16"
2011

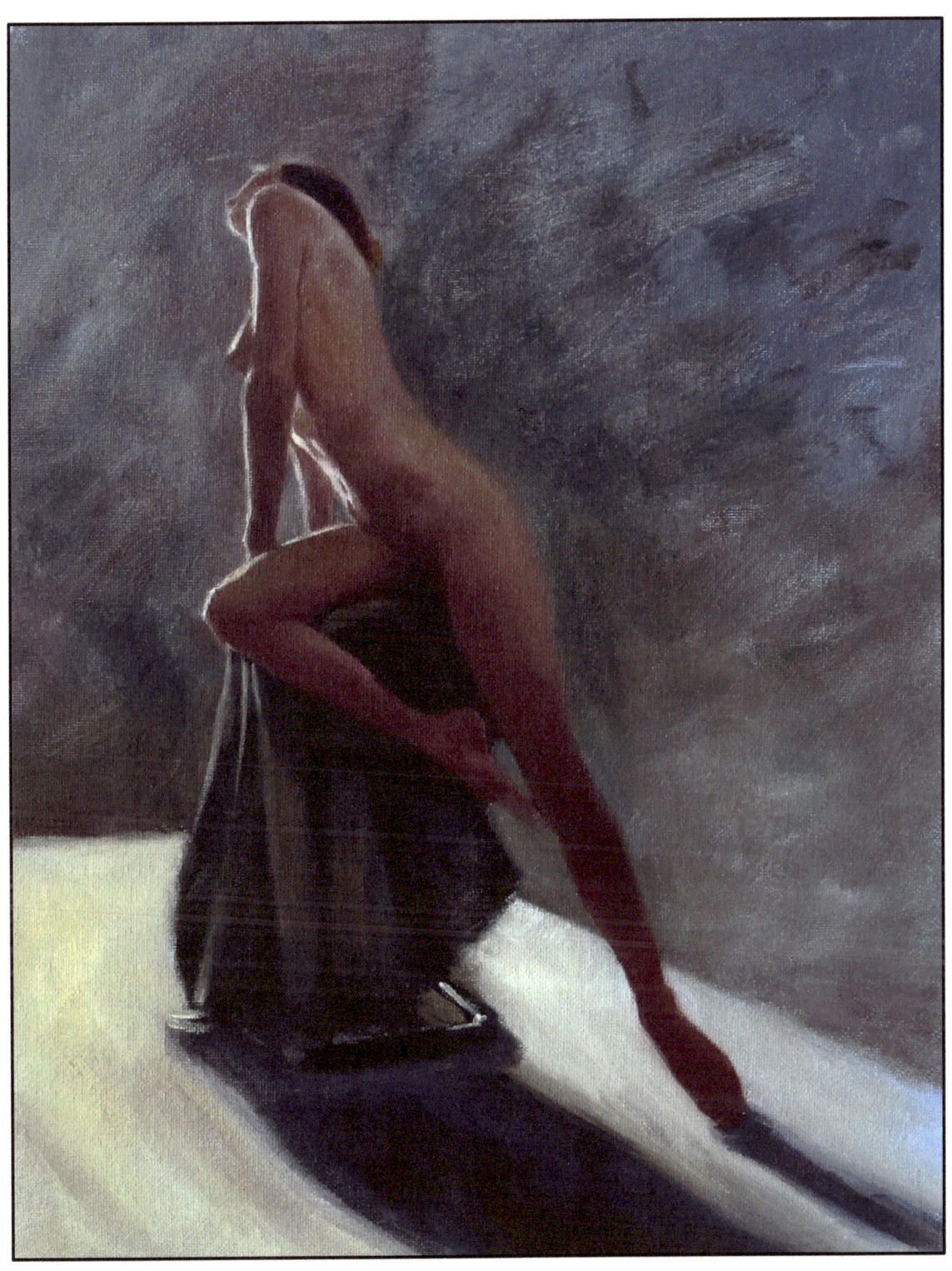

Point of Balance
oil on board
11" x 14"
2012

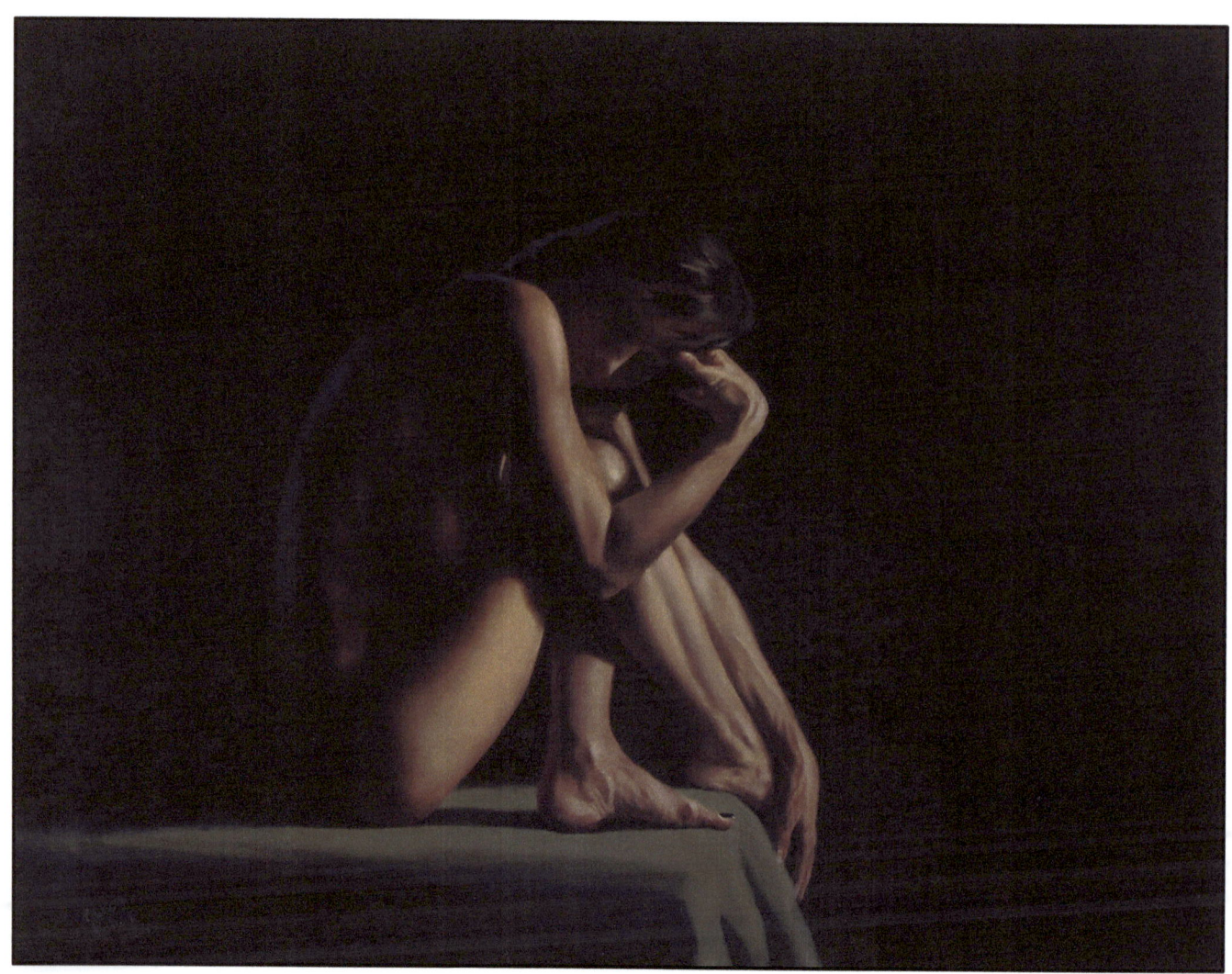

Consumed
oil on board
18" x 24"
2014

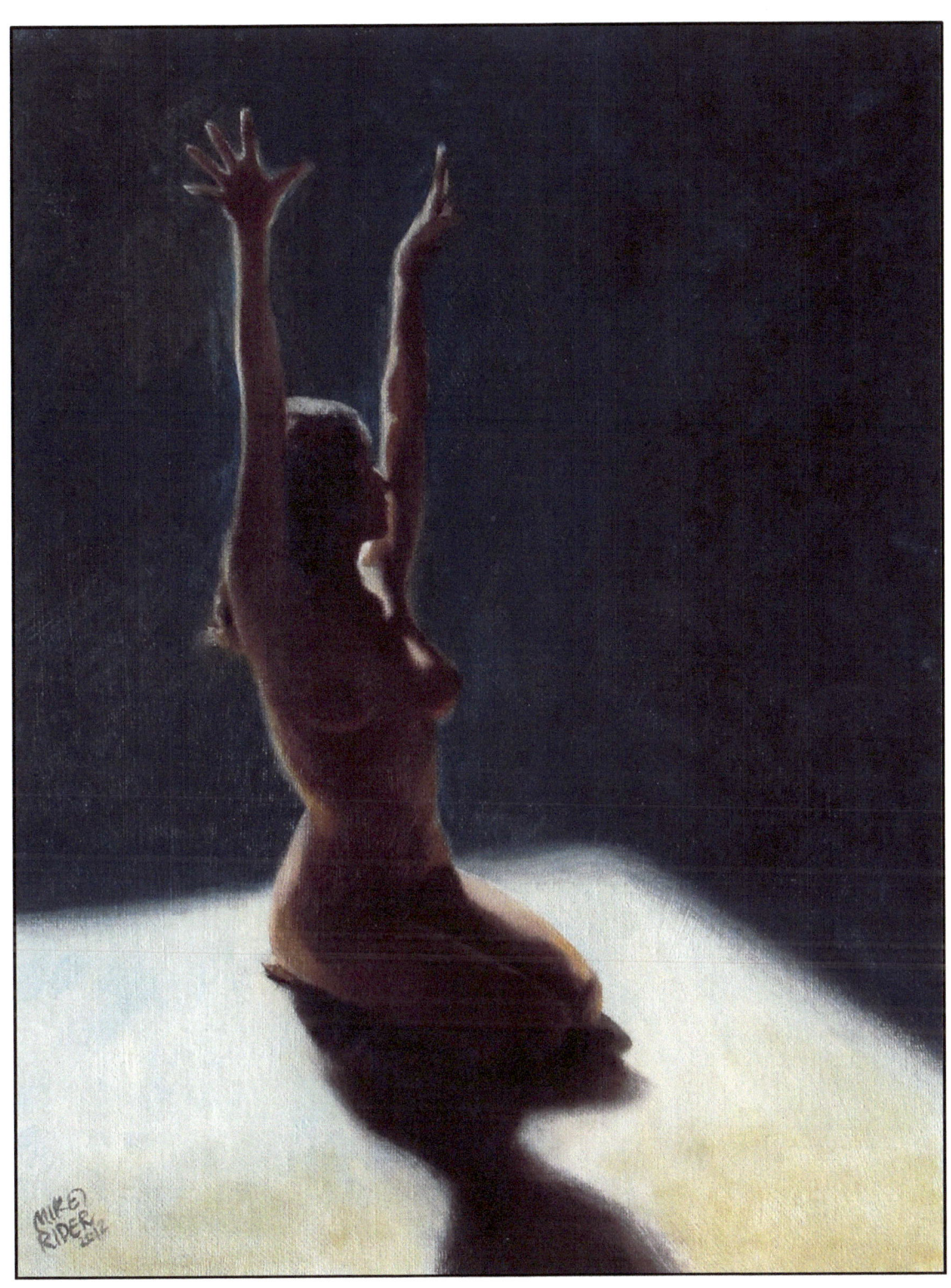

Invocation
oil on board
11" x 14"
2012

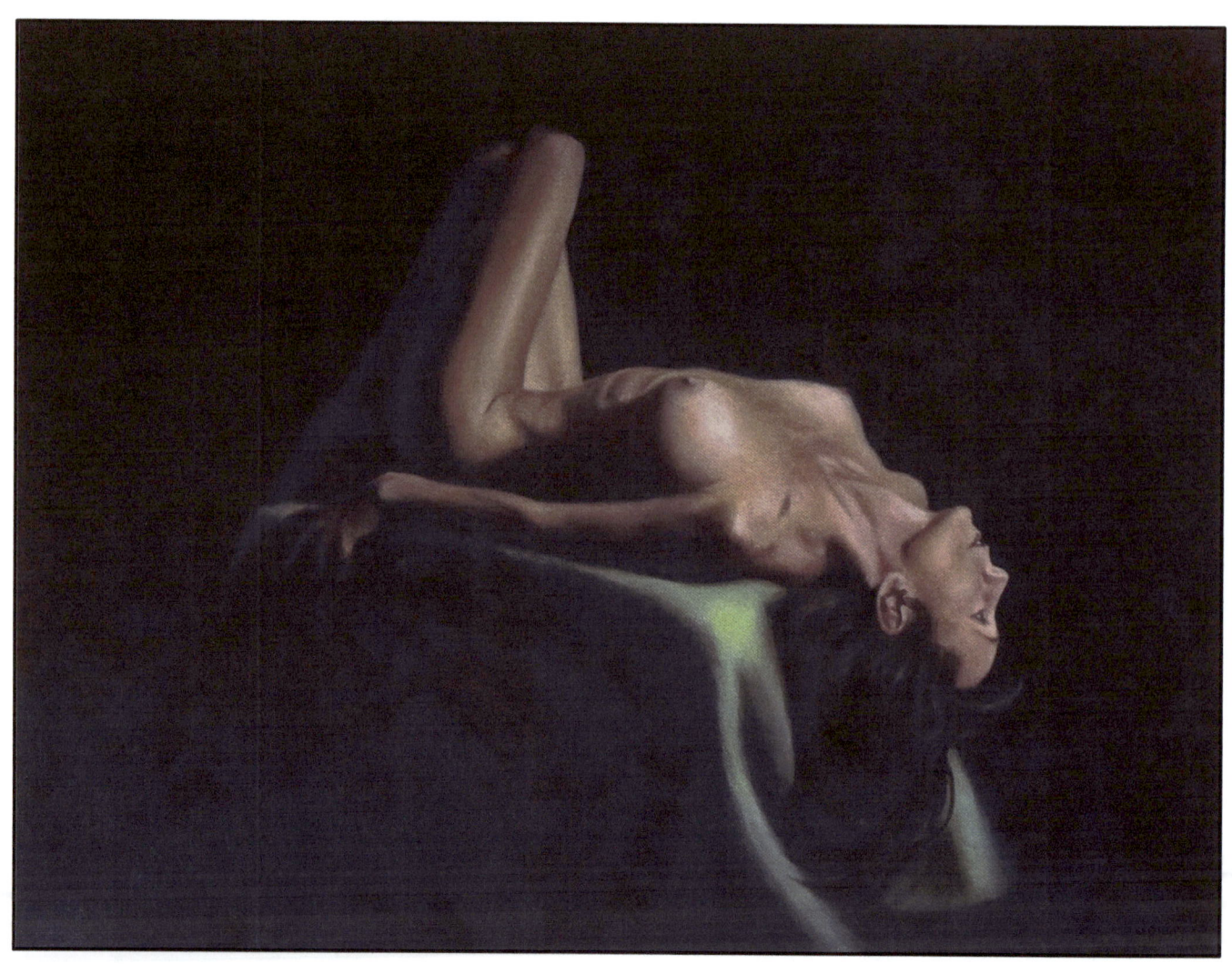

Ephemeral Tranquility
oil on board
18" x 24"
2013

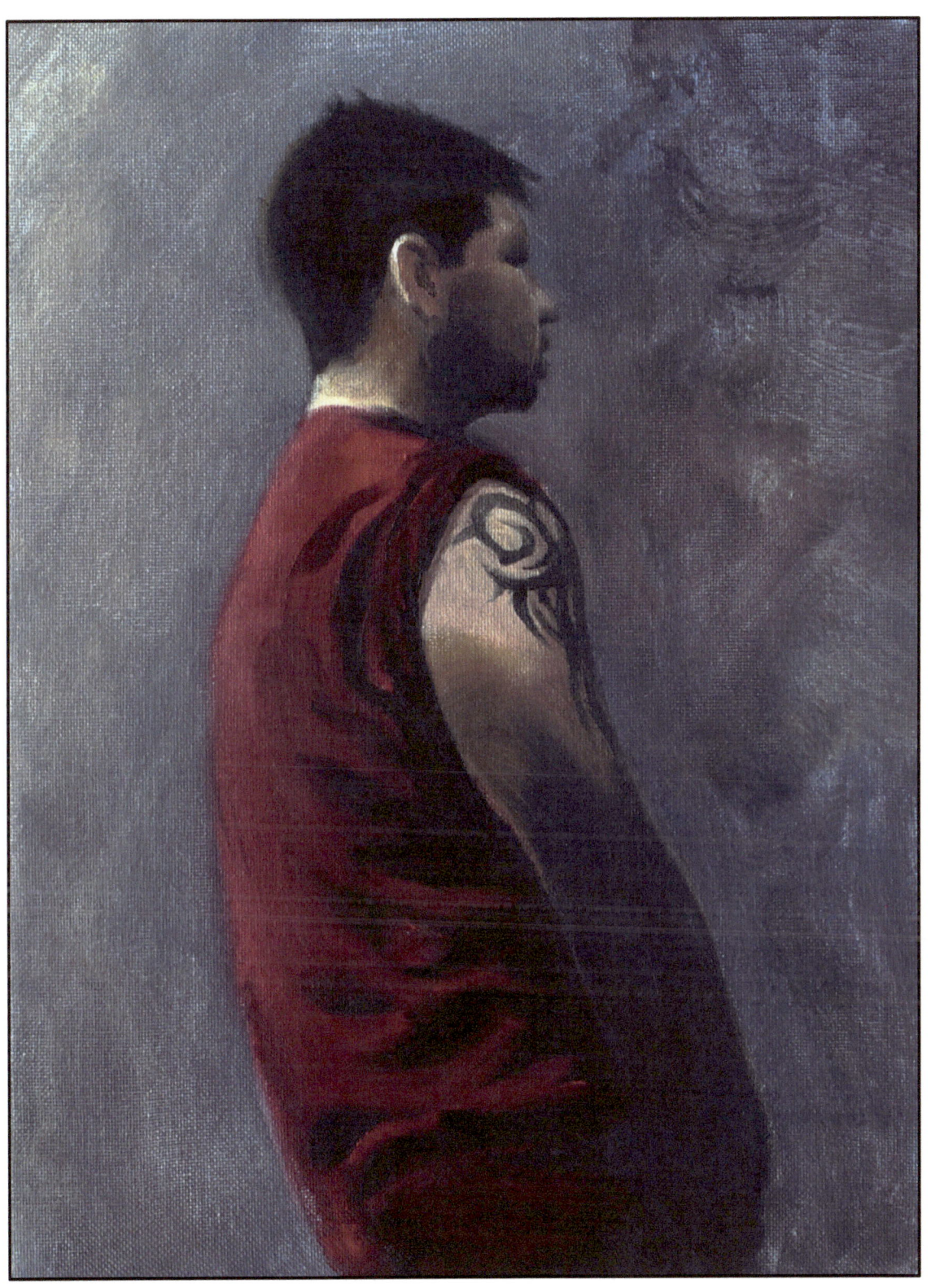

Epiphany
oil on board
12" x 9"
2012

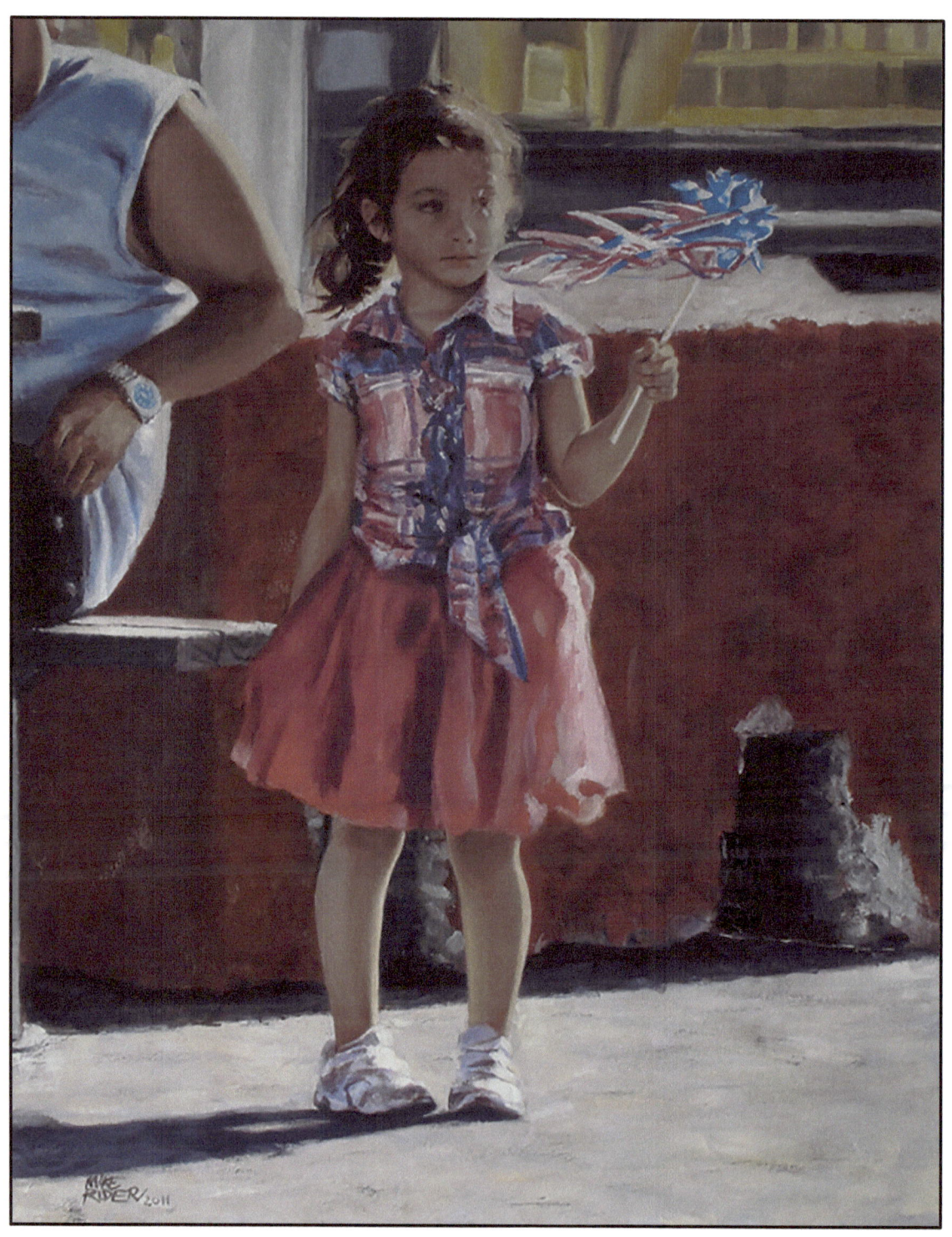

Just Thinking
oil on board
20" x 16"
2011

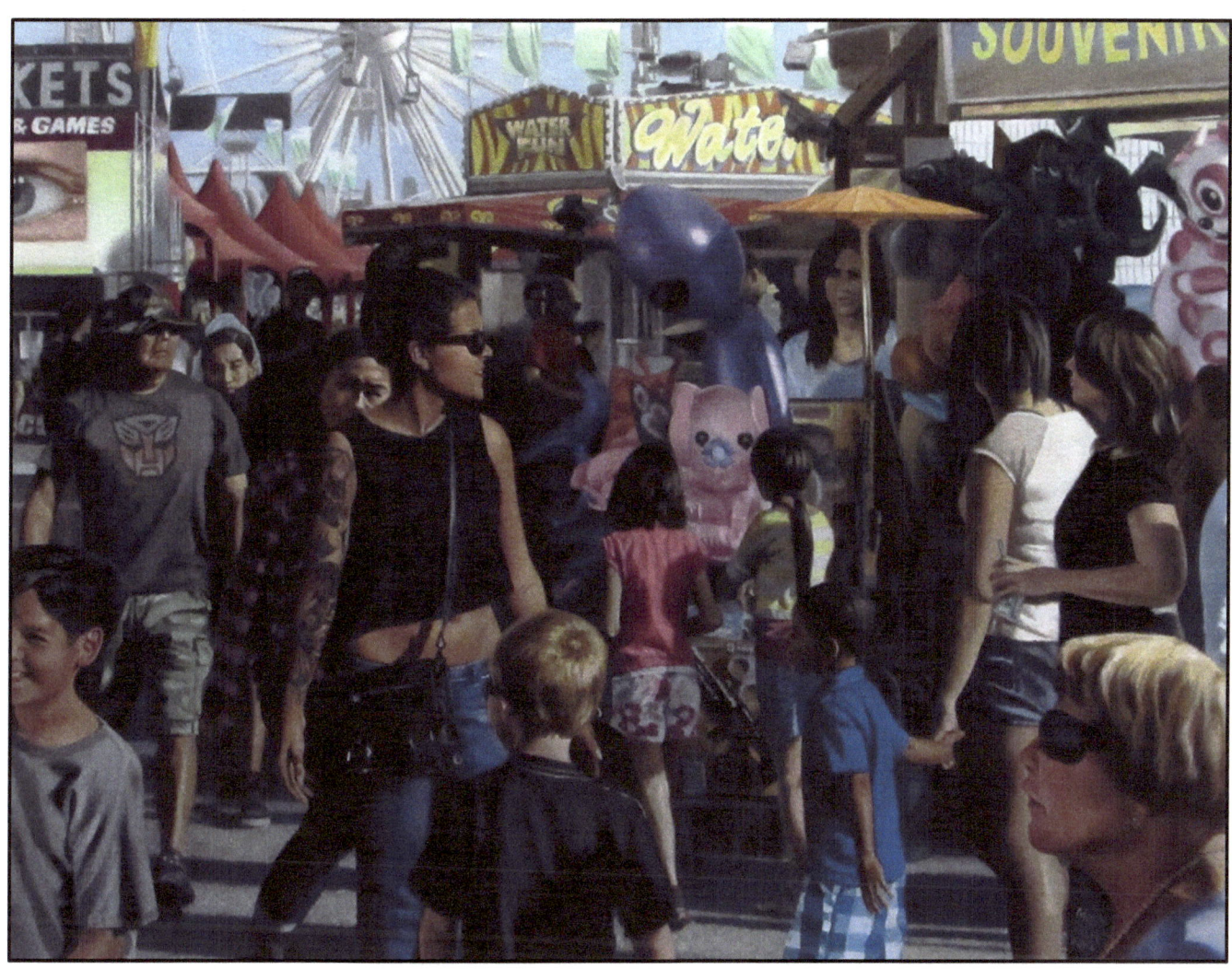

Fearless
oil on board
18" x 24"
2014

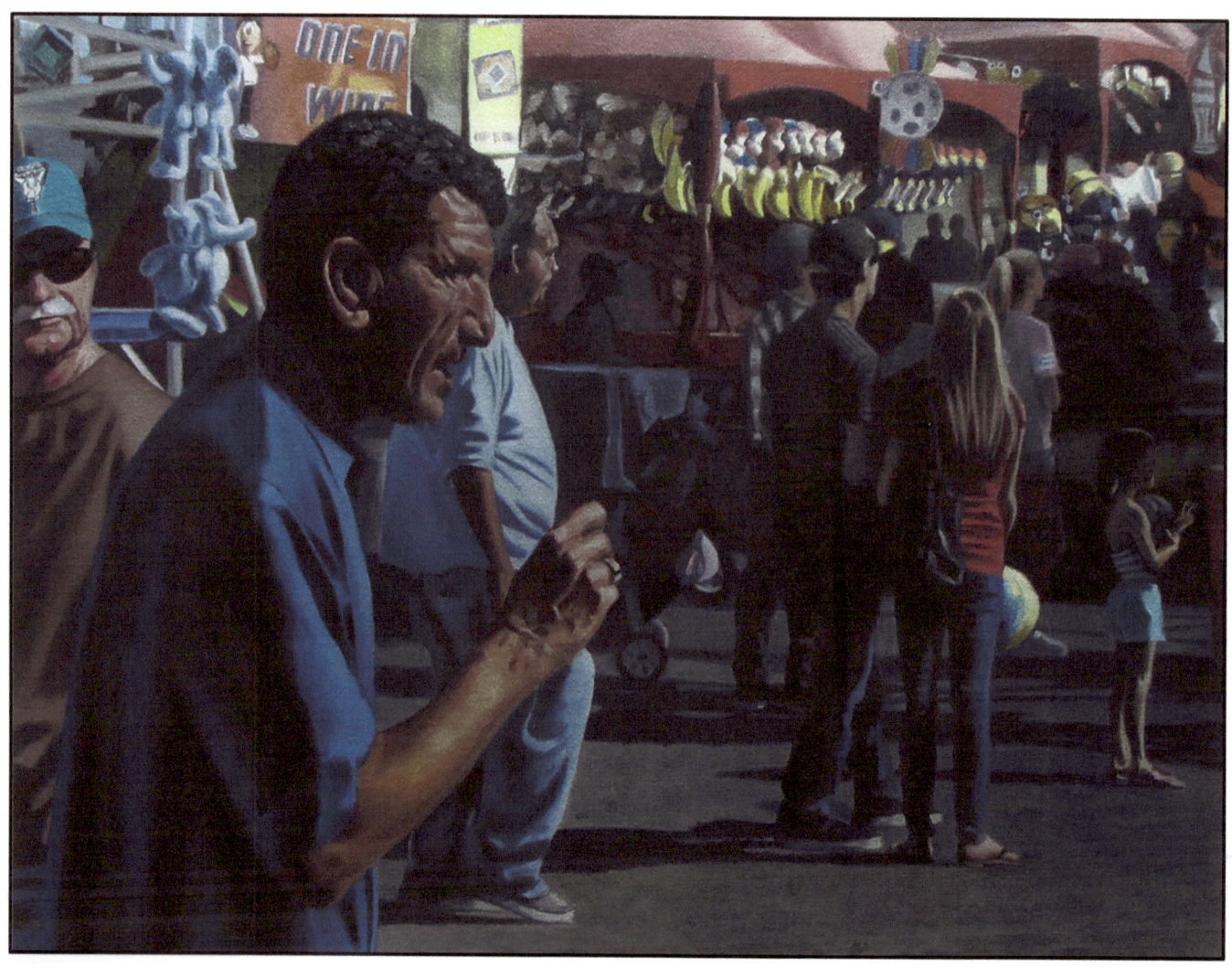

One In Wins
oil on board
18" x 24"
2013

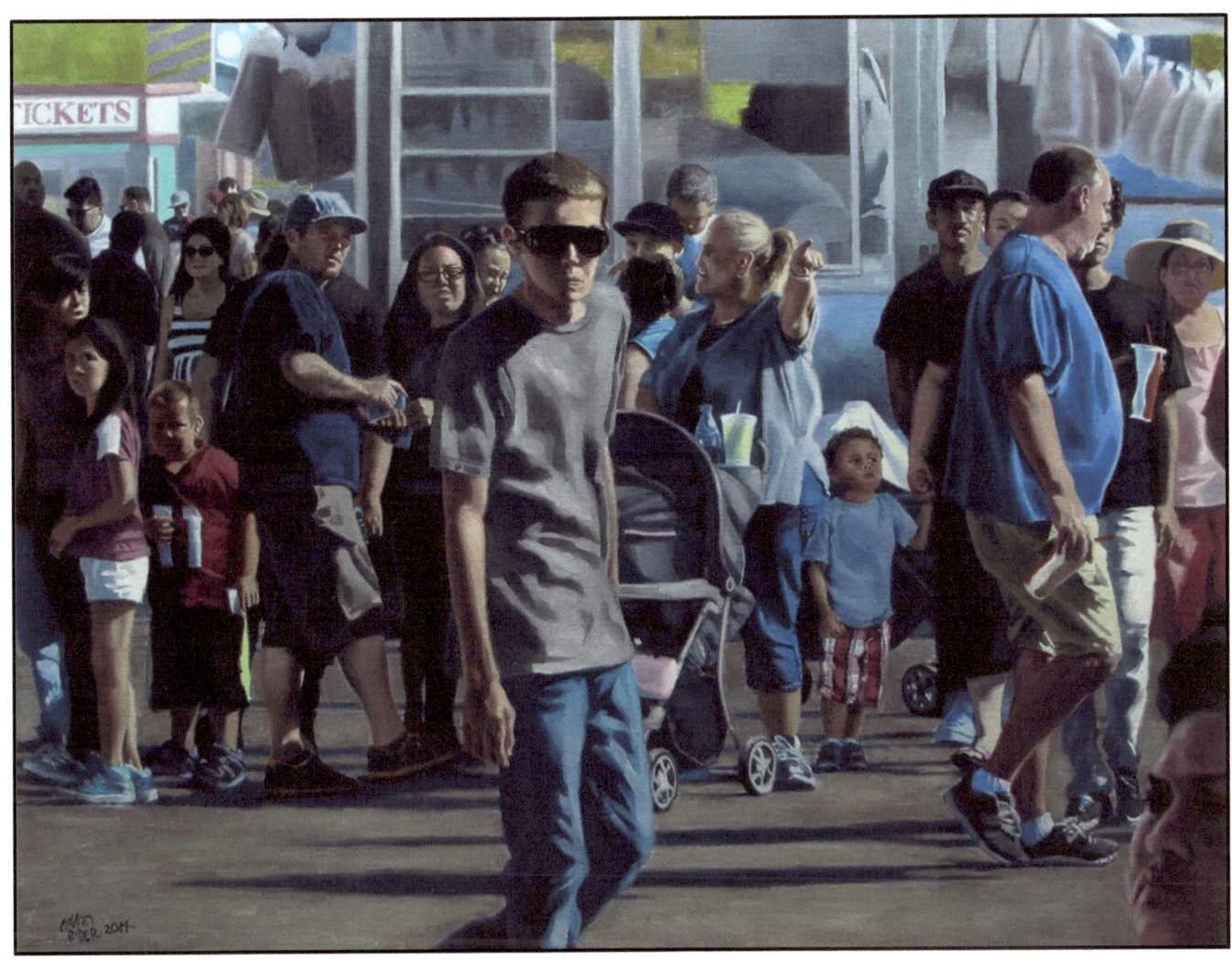

Closer Look
oil on board
18" x 24"
2014

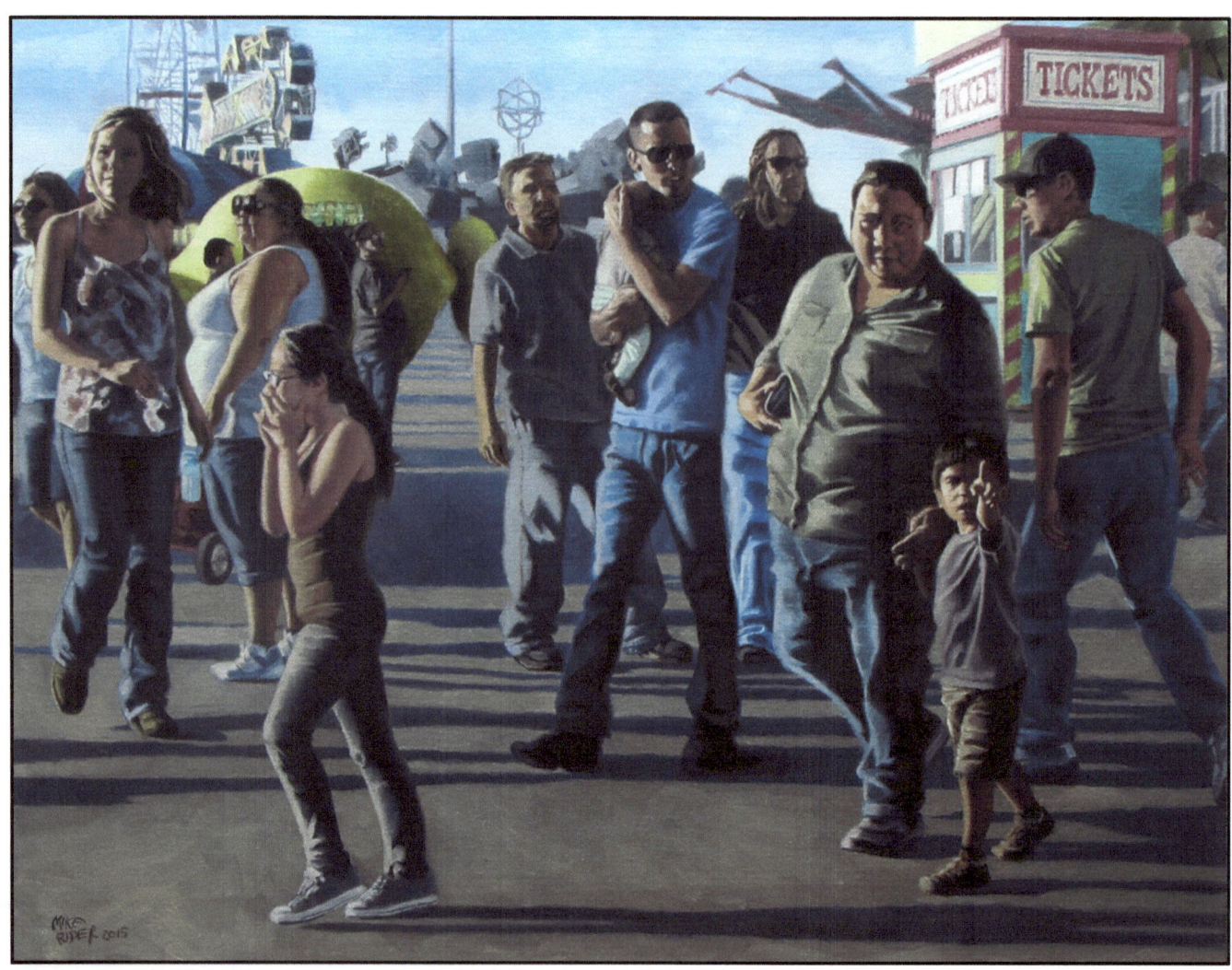

How it Started
oil on board
18" x 24"
2015

Biography

Mike has lived in California and Pennsylvania. He currently resides in Arizona.

Mike received his BFA in drawing from Arizona State University in Tempe, Arizona.

He received his MFA in painting from Academy of Art University in San Francisco, California.

Mike is known primarily for his fine art paintings and drawings. They may be seen on his website, http://www.mikeriderart.com and his Facebook page, https://www.facebook.com/MikeRiderArt.

Mike was a character animation artist at Fox Animation Studios and a key animation artist at Anvil Studios in Phoenix, Arizona on the following animated feature films:

Anastasia (named individually in film credits) film nominated for an Academy Award.

Bartok the Magnificent (named individually in film credits).

Titan AE (named individually in film credits)

Prince Of Egypt (Fox studio named in film credits)

Eight Crazy Nights (Anvil studio named in film credits)

Spirit (Anvil studio named in film credits)

Harvey Birdman: Attorney At Law (named individually in TV credits)

Mike's online IMDB listings may be found under Mike Rider, Michael Rider, and Mike Ryder.

In 2014 Mike began writing and illustrating children's books. His books are available for purchase online: *Squirbly Dreams, Squirbly Dreams Coloring and Activity Book, Rêves de Squirbly" – in French and English,* and *Otis the Jumping Hairy Eyeball.*

Mike is currently at work writing and illustrating more children's books, painting, drawing, and teaching art.

Mike Rider Paintings and Drawings Kindle edition is also available on Amazon.com.
- ASIN: B016VAQQZK

NOTE: Mike Rider's Kindle book versions are free to those who have purchased the paperback edition of the book through the Amazon web site.

Other books by **Mike Rider:**

"Otis, The Jumping Hairy Eyeball"
- ASIN: B010KPUMMA – Kindle edition
- ISBN-10: 151475276X – Paperback edition
- ISBN-13: 978-1514752760 – Paperback edition

Otis is a jumping hairy eyeball. This story follows Otis' silly adventures as he eats jumping beans and jumps all over the world.

"Squirbly Dreams"
- ASIN-B00RH9X4BY – Kindle edition
- ISBN-10: 1505790247 – Paperback edition
- ISBN-13: 978-1505790245 – Paperback edition

A visually stimulating story with frogs, elephants, penguins, dogs, ladybugs, roadrunners, bears, turtles, roly-polies, alligators, whales, monkeys, fish, birds, aliens, inchworms, lobsters...and the list goes on! *Squirbly* is a young frog who frequently dreams when he goes to sleep at night. This story explores the wonder of *Squirbly's* dreams and encourages children to look forward to positive dream adventures as they fall asleep.

"Squirbly Dreams Coloring and Activity Book" – in paperback *only*
- ISBN-10: 1505789893
- ISBN-13: 978-1505789898

This coloring book contains the complete Squirbly Dreams story in black and white with text for children of all ages to color. Additional coloring pages and activities are also included.

"Rêves de Squirbly" – in French and English
- ASIN: B00T3PMCM2– Kindle edition
- ISBN-13: 978-1507807453– Paperback edition
- ISBN-10: 1507807457– Paperback edition

www.ingramcontent.com/pod-product-compliance
Lightning Source LLC
Chambersburg PA
CBHW040744200526
45159CB00023B/1689